VOICING THE EAGLE

VOICING THE EAGLE

A True Story of Courage and Valor

Amanda Matti

OPEN ROAD
INTEGRATED MEDIA
NEW YORK

Copyright © 2017 by Amanda Matti

ISBN: 978-1-5040-8557-1

This edition published in 2023 by Open Road Integrated Media, Inc.
180 Maiden Lane
New York, NY 10038
www.openroadmedia.com

VOICING THE EAGLE

PREFACE

"Take cover!" Major Warren screamed as echoes of AK-47 and small arms fire rung out across the field.

The Marines hit the ground as bullets rained down on their position from an indeterminate location. Sergeant Juarez and the unit's Iraqi translator, Fahdi, dropped to the ground, but it was too late. Before Fahdi's knees hit the grass, he was struck with a searing pain in his chest and was knocked back several feet. In an instant, he was flat on his back staring up at the crystalline blue sky. It felt like he'd been hit by a truck. The air was sucked out of his lungs and he gasped to catch his breath. Sergeant Juarez threw his body protectively over Fahdi's attempting to shield him from further wounds, but as Juarez's weight fell on top of Fahdi it made it even more difficult for Fahdi to get the air he desperately needed back into his lungs.

Once Fahdi finally caught his breath, he noticed the blood. "I've been shot!" he screamed. "Get off me!" Fahdi struggled to push the massive Marine Sergeant off him. Fahdi was wearing body armor but from the pain he was in and the blood he saw he was sure the bullet had gone through it.

"Stay the fuck down!" Sergeant Juarez yelled back. "I'm hit! It went through!" Fahdi continued to yell and squirm under

Juarez's weight. Due to the immense pain and trouble he was having to breathe, Fahdi feared the bullet had struck one of his lungs.

Sergeant Juarez sat up and straddled Fahdi, holding him down so he could survey the damage. "Where are you hit?" he yelled.

"My chest!" Fahdi blurted. Blood was smeared all over the front of Fahdi's uniform and across his body armor. "Oh fuck! Oh fuck! I'm bleeding bad!" He was in a lot of pain but actually relieved because he knew the pain meant he probably wasn't dying. Sergeant Juarez ripped the Velcro straps from Fahdi's bullet proof vest and pushed the armor up over his head. He ran his hands up and down Fahdi's chest and stomach and across his shoulders.

"There's nothing! It didn't go through. You're fine."

"But I'm bleeding!" Fahdi argued.

"No, you're not. I am," Juarez replied in a surprisingly calm tone.

Fahdi looked and saw Sergeant Juarez's uniform near the top corner of his right shoulder was ripped. Blood was seeping from the area and dripping down his arm. He'd been grazed by a round, perhaps the same one that took Fahdi down. When he'd thrown his body over Fahdi's, he bled onto him, covering Fahdi in more blood than himself. "Shit dude, you're hit!" Fahdi said, now shifting his focus from his own injuries to Sergeant Juarez's shoulder wound. "We've gotta' get you to a medic."

"It's fine. It looks worse than it really is. I only got grazed," Juarez said as he grabbed Fahdi's vest and looked at it. His finger found the indentation where the AK-47 round that took Fahdi down was embedded deep into one of the vest's chest plates. "See," he said pointing it out to Fahdi, "the bullet that got you is right here. Put your vest back on, we've got to catch back up with the Major."

Fahdi pulled the body armor vest back over his head and strapped it on. He glanced down and noticed the bullet was lodged in the area right over his heart. *Holy fuck! I'd have been dead.*

CHAPTER ONE

ABANDON SHIP

JANUARY–MARCH 2003

"I don't give a shit *who* you are, you're not coming in until I get clearance from Central Security authorizing you to enter this palace."

It was January 2003 and twenty-one-year-old Fahdi was on duty as a palace security guard at the Al Dora Farms compound outside Baghdad, one of former Iraqi President Saddam Hussein's smaller palaces he had gifted to his daughter. Fahdi had been serving as a lower-level security guard for nearly a year, rotating several days a week to different palaces and government residences throughout Baghdad.

"I was basically a rent-a-cop," Fahdi explained to me ten years later as we sat on the large front porch of our rural Ohio home. My iPhone sat between us on a small patio table with the voice recorder app engaged. Halfway through a Marlboro cigarette, smoke swirling above his head, he maintained a thousand-yard stare out across the ocean of corn crops blanketing the fields surrounding our house. The Midwest summer sun was setting before him, transforming the smoke into an ethereal manifestation, moving and dancing with its own personality around his dark silhouette.

Like most of the middle-and upper-class teens in Baghdad, at age fifteen, Fahdi was drafted into the Youth Union headed by Saddam Hussein's infamous son, Uday. A cross between the Boy Scouts and the YMCA, the union was an organization designed to cultivate a strong sense of nationalism and loyalty to Saddam, his family, and the Ba'athist regime amongst the youth of Baghdad. Fahdi had excelled as a member of the Youth Union, quickly progressing beyond the basic club activities, and moving up the ranks into the upper echelons of the organization that offered paid positions and even full-fledged career paths in the areas of government security, community organizing, and other social service professions throughout Iraq's capital city and beyond. Although most these positions were reserved for individuals who were related to either Saddam's family or other senior government officials, Fahdi was the next best thing, Christian.

It's a common misconception that Christians in Iraq were persecuted and oppressed under Saddam's regime. The reality for many Christian families in Baghdad was quite the opposite. Saddam trusted Christians above many Muslim Arabs who were not blood-related to him, knowing they would never be a threat to his power due to their small minority. Christians often held high-level security positions and were employed as palace chefs and housecleaning staff; even one of Saddam's closest advisors and foreign ministers, Tariq Aziz, was a Catholic.

Fahdi worked part-time with the palace security detail while attending Baghdad University, where he was an English Language major.

"Practically everyone's goal after high school was to attend either the Engineering College or Medical School to become a doctor. I checked out both of those schools but ultimately decided the College of Languages was right for me. It had the highest percentage of hot chicks," Fahdi said with a sly smile.

He'd received word from his bosses at the palace security forces "some people" may be stopping by the Al-Dora Farms palace that chilly January day, but typically it only meant a couple of workers to perhaps fix a toilet or repair a broken window. The person standing before him now, demanding entry into the palace grounds, was an Iraqi man flashing an Iraqi Intelligence Service badge identifying him as Officer Malwood. Behind him were fifteen foreigners, either European or American, sitting in four SUVs adorned with recognizable insignias—The United Nations.

"Just open the gate son," Malwood said in a patronizing tone, looking at Fahdi through the large iron gates of the palace wall. "These are official UN inspectors and we have clearance to enter the compound and have been authorized to look around inside the palace."

"That's all well and good, but I'm still not opening this gate until I receive explicit instructions from my supervisors to let you in," Fahdi replied.

"Listen here, you little shit," Malwood spat back, "you will do as I say. I outrank you!"

"With all due respect, not while I'm on the other side of this gate you don't," Fahdi replied as calmly as possible, although nervous a hell.

"If you do not open these gates this instant, not only will I make sure you lose this job, I'll make sure they cut off your balls and shove them in your mouth before chopping off your head!"

Fahdi knew the United Nations was currently roaming the country conducting weapons inspections at Saddam's palaces, but many of the rumors coming through were that American CIA members were also posing as UN Inspectors to infiltrate Iraq's sensitive government locations. Fahdi wanted to ensure he covered all his bases before granting them access or it'd be his ass.

Fahdi told Malwood to wait in his vehicle while he contacted Central Security to obtain official authorization for them to enter the compound. He headed to the communications shack and tried to reach his supervisors via phone—no answer. There were three other security guards on duty with Fahdi and the four of them conferred to decide how to handle the situation.

"You speak English Fahdi. Are those people out there really with the United Nations?" one of his fellow guards asked.

"They're definitely speaking English, but I don't know where they're from. All I know is none of us is saying a word to any of them until we get orders."

"We were all scared shitless. We didn't want to cause any issues by not letting the inspectors in. It was common knowledge not to fuck with the UN, but we'd also heard stories of one of the palace guards at another location who got in serious trouble for allowing the inspectors in and showing them things he wasn't supposed to show them."

In the end, they all agreed it was safer not to let the inspectors in and piss them off than to let them in and feel the merciless hand of Central Security.

Finally, nearly an hour after the inspectors arrived, the phone in the palace communications shack rang. Fahdi answered it and was given permission from the Assistant Chief of Central Security to allow Malwood and the UN inspectors to enter the Al-Dora compound. "Let them in and let them see and do whatever they want," the Assistant Chief instructed Fahdi. "If they want to dig holes, let them dig. If they want to knock down walls, let them have at it. Whatever they want to do. You got it?"

"Yes, sir, I understand. I didn't mean to cause any trouble, I just wanted to be sure before I—"

The Assistant Chief cut him off. "You're not in any trouble. You were right to wait for our confirmation."

Fahdi breathed a huge sigh of relief, then opened the gate. Malwood, still seething and wanting to ring his neck, flashed a fake smile and feigned an amiable mood for the UN inspectors.

Once parked inside the gates, the UN inspectors climbed from their vehicles and broke into three groups. Fahdi made sure a palace guard accompanied each group. Fahdi never spoke a word of English to the Inspectors and, clearly, Malwood's English was practically non-existent. The UN team had their own translator with them who did all the communicating between the inspectors and the Iraqis. Nevertheless, Fahdi listened intently to every word the inspectors in his group said. The groups moseyed at a leisurely pace around the palace, opening random doors and taking quick looks inside some rooms while walking right past others.

"It felt more like they were interested home buyers walking through a neighborhood open house instead of UN inspectors searching for weapons of mass destruction."

One of the inspectors in each group carried a gadget of some sort Fahdi believed was used to measure radiation levels in the air, but their demeanor made it clear they didn't expect to find anything at that particular palace.

As Fahdi began escorting his group back toward the front of the compound, the palace chef intercepted the group and informed Fahdi he'd received a call instructing him and his crew to prepare lunch for the "guests."

Son-of-a-bitch! We have to feed these assholes, too? Fahdi directed everyone to the dining room where the inspectors and

Malwood spent the next two hours laughing and joking while dining on lamb and rice.

Fahdi and the other palace guards stood quietly in the shadows thinking to themselves, *Holy shit, are these people ever going to leave?*

Finally, the UN team leader glanced at his watch and was visibly surprised by the late hour. He announced they really needed to be getting on their way as the sun was beginning to set; that they had to be back to wherever they were staying before dark.

As the UN vehicles disappeared into a cloud of dust, Fahdi called Central Security and told the Assistant Chief the inspectors had departed.

"I need you and the other guards to each write fully-detailed reports of everything the inspectors and their Iraqi Intelligence escort did during their visit," the Assistant Chief instructed. "I want to know what they said, what they saw, where they went, what they ate, everything. If they used the bathroom, it better be in the report how long they were in there and if they took a shit or pissed. You got it?"

Even though Fahdi spoke English and understood almost every word the inspectors said, he still wasn't sure what to put in the report.

"I was afraid they'd be disappointed because nothing interesting or really noteworthy happened. Each time we directed the inspectors into one of the palace rooms, all they could say was, 'Wow! This is absolutely beautiful.' So, my report essentially read: We walked into a room and they said, 'Wow.' We walked into another room and they said, 'Wow.'"

A couple of days later, Fahdi and the other three guards on duty with him at Al-Dora during the UN inspection were ordered to report to Central Security Command. The Assistant

Chief had them all sit in front of a television and pressed play on a VCR. It was a recording of a newscast that had recently come across one of the twenty-four-hour European news outlets. According to the report, the UN had recently reported being blocked for several hours from entering one of the palaces in the Al-Dora area on the outskirts of Baghdad, and it was suspected the officials inside the palace were using that time to destroy incriminating evidence pointing to Iraq's harboring of WMDs or perhaps hiding actual weapons.

"Are you fucking kidding me?" Fahdi protested, immediately fearing they were in deep shit.

"This is total bullshit!" another guard said.

"All those fuckers did was come in and marvel at the damn closet space and the pretty bathrooms!" Fahdi declared.

"Then they ate all our food," the other guard added. "The news report failed to mention they spent twice as much time enjoying lunch as they did 'inspecting' anything."

"Everyone calm down," the Assistant Chief piped in. "No one's in trouble, I just thought you boys would be interested in seeing this. We feel you handled everything well and did what you were supposed to do. Everyone knows the Americans own the Western media and were going to say whatever the U.S. tells them to say. But it's clear the inspectors aren't interested in learning the truth. They're simply here as a front to give the U.S. a false edict to eventually declare war. There will be an official order going out to the entire Palace Guard: no one is to allow any more UN inspectors into any of the compounds. Dismissed."

A little over a month later, Fahdi was on security duty at a palace in Saddam's hometown of Tikrit, approximately 250 km north of Baghdad; one much larger than the al-Dora compound and belonged to Uday Hussein. The Palace Guard referred to it as the

13

"Island Palace" as it was situated on a ten-acre peninsula jutting out into the Tigris River. The palace itself was over 10,000 square feet with twelve bedrooms and separate quarters on the outskirts of the premises where the palace staff and security detail, which was typically comprised of six palace guards, stayed while on duty.

Two days before U.S. President George Bush appeared on television making his famous speech, giving Saddam and his sons forty-eight hours to surrender before the U.S. officially invaded, Fahdi and the five other palace guards on duty with him were eating dinner in the guard house discussing the impending war with America. None of the six thought the U.S. would really invade Iraq with ground forces.

"It'll probably just be like the cruise missile bombings Clinton did in '96," one of the guards commented as he stuffed a handful of lamb and rice in his mouth.

"Yeah, probably a few smart bombs and then everything will go back to normal," another added.

"I don't know. They seem damn pissed since the 9/11 attacks," a third chimed in. "George Bush doesn't seem like he's fucking around. They've been bombing the shit out of Afghanistan for the past year."

"But none of the terrorists on 9/11 were Iraqi," Fahdi said. "We had nothing to do with it and don't have any ties with Al-Qaeda. Why the hell would they come after us?"

As the world knows, Bush made good on his promise. On March 20, 2003, approximately ninety minutes after the lapse of the forty-eight-hour deadline, bombs began falling on Baghdad. And shortly thereafter, ground forces crossed the border from Kuwait into Iraq. The war had started.

Fahdi and the other guards remained at the Island Palace, but communication with Central Security in Baghdad had gone dark the day the invasion started. They all decided to wait it out and stay put until they heard word from higher up. News and information from Baghdad was coming in via phone calls between the palace staff and their families back in the capital city.

The morning after the invasion started, Fahdi managed to get a hold of his younger brother, Fareed, who was in Baghdad with their mother and thirteen-year-old sister, Farrah.

"So far, it seems they're only bombing government buildings and palaces," Fareed relayed over the phone. "But we are going to go ahead and head north to the village. Mom is packing now."

Fahdi and his siblings were all born in Baghdad and had lived in the city all their lives, but Fahdi's parents were originally from a small Christian village in Northern Iraq, outside Mosul near the Kurdish region. Fahdi's grandparents and most of his extended family still lived in the village, and his family visited often. Fahdi had spent many holiday breaks and summer days running across the green hillsides of the rural village. It was a perfect location to wait out U.S. bombings of Baghdad. The family had been forced to go there on several occasions since Fahdi was a small child.

"Do you want to come with us?" Fahdi's brother asked him. "Since they are bombing palaces, they'll probably start going after ones outside of Baghdad soon, especially in Tikrit. We can stop and pick you up on our way north."

"No, I have to stay," Fahdi replied solemnly. "If I abandon my post, we'll have to pray the Americans burn this country to the ground or it'll be my ass."

"Okay, but promise me you won't be a martyr."

"Don't worry, I'm not that loyal," Fahdi replied, jokingly.

As the aerial bombardment of Baghdad continued—the infamous "shock and awe" stage of the invasion—thousands of civilians fled the city and many came through Tikrit on their way north. One of the guards or other staff at the Island Palace would periodically drive into Tikrit to gather information on what was happening in Baghdad from the people passing through. Rumor had it, the Americans and British were fighting to take Iraq's largest southern city, Basra, and U.S. ground forces were moving toward Baghdad, which was somewhat accurate.

Every hour, Fahdi or one of the other security guards tried calling Central Security in Baghdad, but all they got was a consistent busy tone.

A few days after the invasion began, Fahdi heard the distinct whirring sound of incoming cruise missiles overhead. The U.S. began bombing known military bases around Tikrit, but everyone in the Island Palace knew it was only a matter of time before they were on the menu. The staff—cooks, the cleaning crew, gardeners, etc.—all abandoned the Island Palace the day after the bombings in Tikrit started, but Fahdi and the other palace guards remained behind. If they fled, and the Americans decided to pack up and go home before the country fell, they'd be dead men for disserting. They felt secure in the guard quarters, about 100 meters from the main house. Should the Americans decide to target the Island Palace, they'd probably drop a bomb smack in the center of it.

After clearing the palace of provisions and relocating supplies to the guard quarters, they refrained from going anywhere near the main house. Information coming in from Baghdad was growing bleaker by the hour. Word on the street was the government had all but collapsed and top officials had gone underground or were on the run. Nearly two weeks after communications went dark with Central Security, Fahdi and the other guards decided to discuss their options.

"I think it's time for us to go guys," Harith, one of the guards, said, and a couple of the others nodded in agreement. "We haven't heard a word from Central Security in days. The government is gone and the Americans are about to take Baghdad. They'll shoot us where we stand if we're still here when they come to take this place."

Fahdi remained silent, not convinced the government was completely gone and feared what his Iraqi supervisors would do to him for disserting his post more than what the Americans may do to him should they show up.

"Fahdi, man, what are you thinking?" one of the guards asked, noticing Fahdi's silence. "You're awfully quiet."

"I'm not leaving," Fahdi responded shaking his head. "Not until someone above me either calls or personally comes and tells me to leave. If we get caught abandoning our post, they will execute us."

"There's no one left!" Harith retorted. "It's all over! I'm leaving tonight and anyone who wants to leave, too, is welcome to join me."

Around midnight, four of the guards left, leaving Fahdi and one other guard, Saif, alone at the Island Palace. The two took turns calling Central Security every fifteen minutes, but the busy signal continued. Another missile whirred overhead across the night sky and connected with its target in a massive explosion just a few kilometers from the them.

"I'm beginning to think we should have left with the others," Saif said in a somber tone.

"I'm beginning to think you're right," Fahdi agreed. "Let me make one more phone call."

"No one's there, man. Central Security has been abandoned. I'm sure of it now."

"I'm not calling them," Fahdi replied and dialed the number of his next-door neighbor in Baghdad, Waleed, who was a senior level official in the Ministry of Foreign Affairs. He hoped to learn a little more about the state of the government from him before making a final decision. "It's ringing," Fahdi exclaimed, excited to hear something other than a busy tone. He closed his eyes in relief at the sound of Waleed's voice on the other end.

"Waleed, it's Fahdi, from next door."

"Fahdi? Are you home?" Waleed asked confused. "I thought I just saw your family leaving."

"They did. I'm not with them. I'm on duty at the Island Palace. We can't get a hold of Central Security. We haven't heard anything from them in two weeks and we were wondering . . . I mean, we're not sure . . ."

"Leave *now*," Waleed replied plainly, understanding Fahdi was fishing for some sort of permission or reason to abandon his post.

"But, what if—"

"*Leave now!*" Waleed reiterated more firmly. "And if anyone asks, you can tell them I told you to leave. But trust me, no one's going to ask, ever."

"Okay, we will," Fahdi replied, half-relieved and half-distressed.

"But don't come back to Baghdad," Waleed advised. "It's literally a warzone here. I'm on the way out myself. They're bombing the shit out of us and ground forces are on their way. It's over. Good luck, my friend."

"Good luck to you, too." And with that, Fahdi hung up the phone.

"Saif, get your stuff. We're leaving."

"Thank God," Saif muttered under his breath.

The two gathered their personal belongings, along with any food and supplies that were easy to pack, and stuffed everything in the backseat of Fahdi's car. They did their best to secure the compound, double-checking every window, door, and gate to ensure they were locked.

"Did you make sure the kitchen doors around back were locked?" Fahdi asked before they got in the car.

"Everything's locked."

"Are you sure?"

"Yes."

"Go double check anyway. I'm going to check the front again." Fahdi doubled-timed it toward the front of the palace.

Saif huffed at Fahdi's nagging but went around back to check the kitchen doors again. The two met back up at the car and decided they'd done all they could. Time to abandon ship.

Fahdi slipped into the driver's seat of his BMW sedan and Saif climbed in on the passenger side. They exchanged a brief silent glance, then Fahdi turned the ignition. Clearing the massive iron gates of the palace's front entrance, Fahdi brought the car to a quick halt. He hopped out and pulled the gates closed, securing them with a padlock. As it clicked, he took one last look at the Island Palace, looming in the shadows, and inhaled deeply. He knew once he climbed back in the car and drove away, there would be no turning back. He'd officially be a deserter. A traitor to his country. A wanted man by whatever Iraqi government remained come daybreak.

Fahdi and Saif were only a few hundred yards down the road when the missile struck. Fahdi watched as the Island Palace exploded into a ball of flames and dust in his rearview mirror.

"Well, it's a good thing we made sure all the doors were locked," Saif said sarcastically as he and Fahdi hauled ass.

Fahdi remained silent, staring at the road ahead with a stony glare. The disintegration of the Island Palace represented what was happening to his country as a whole. The Iraq he had known all his life was quickly burning to the ground.

CHAPTER TWO

BAGHDAD FALLS

APRIL 2003

It's typically a three-hour drive from Tikrit to Fahdi's family village. The night he fled the Island Palace he made it in an hour and a half. After dropping Saif at a friend's house outside Tikrit, Fahdi floored the gas pedal all the way to Mosul. The entire drive, his gaze alternated between the rearview mirror and the road ahead of him; positive at any minute he'd be chased down by Iraqi police or the military coming to arrest him for deserting his post.

Reaching his grandfather's house, he climbed out of his car visibly trembling with fear. His mother rushed out and embraced her eldest child, praising God that he'd made it out of Tikrit unscathed.

Fahdi's paranoia did not subside until they received a phone call a few days later from friends still in Baghdad, reporting American military tanks had infiltrated the city. Less than twenty-four hours later, it was officially announced on TV that Saddam Hussein was no longer in power.

"We were a little skeptical at first because the village is far from Baghdad and out of range of any Baghdad-based news channels. We were only able to get Kurdish news channels, who were itching for Saddam to go down, so it was quite possible they had jumped the gun on reporting his fall from power."

Fahdi didn't completely believe Saddam was truly gone until two days later when, with his own eyes, he witnessed American tanks rolling through downtown Mosul.

"The tanks were intimidating, to say the least. The American M1 Abrams tanks are about three times the size of the Iraqi tanks I was used to seeing. They were like moving buildings."

The U.S. tanks in Mosul had come down from the North via Kurdistan and the Kurdish militia, the Peshmerga, came with them. According to reports, the Iraqi military commander in charge of Mosul surrendered the city to the U.S. without a fight. Many residents of Mosul were acquiescent to the U.S. military presence, but they viewed the Peshmerga as anything but liberators.

Within days of the Kurdish militia's arrival, accounts of the Peshmerga looting banks, mosques, universities, and private businesses across Mosul began to emerge. Bands of Mosul residents appealed to the U.S. forces to put an end to the looting or at least try to curb the rampant pillaging, but the Americans were reluctant to interfere, so the initial acceptance the residents of Mosul had for U.S. troops began transforming into resentment.

Although the situation in Mosul was deteriorating, it was still far superior to conditions in Baghdad. A steady flow of evacuees from the capital city continued to flow into Mosul, bringing stories of mass chaos, destruction, and carnage. The sudden fall of Saddam's government created a massive power vacuum resulting in the city essentially imploding into complete anarchy. With no police or security forces remaining to enforce any measure of law, street gangs quickly formed and began roaming Baghdad, taking anything they could carry away and burning buildings in retreat.

As more accounts of the utter mayhem in Baghdad poured in, Fahdi was anxious to return as soon as possible to make sure his family's business was still standing.

Fahdi had only been ten years old when his father passed away, but thankfully, he'd built a successful veterinary supply business that supported the family after his death. The business imported and sold vaccinations, antibiotics, supplements, vitamins, hormones, etc. for livestock to farmers. He desperately wanted to safeguard his family's livelihood. The business was the main source of income for his widowed mother and younger siblings.

Fahdi and one of his uncles, Marwan, who also lived in Baghdad and had evacuated to the village, decided to return together to check on their homes and businesses. The journey back south was a surreal experience for both. Along the route, the shoulders of the highway were littered with burned out Iraqi Army tanks and random billows of smoke rose across the desert from smoldering buildings, vehicles, and other structures. As they approached the outskirts of Baghdad, the concentration of American troops (mostly Marines), Humvees, tanks, and other military vehicles grew steadily.

Their first stop was Fahdi's family's business. Much to their relief, it was intact and relatively unscathed. From there, the pair continued to Fahdi's house. Aside from a few blown-out windows and a busted front door, the house was fully intact as well. At first, he feared the house had been looted, but nothing was missing. Neighbors later confirmed the damage was the result of an American airstrike that hit so close the residual concussion from the bombs damaged many of the houses in the area.

As they finished evaluating the damage, the sun began to set. Without enough daylight left to make it to Marwan's house and not wanting to be out and about in Baghdad after dark, they decided it best to bed down for the night and check on Marwan's house in the morning.

It was a long sleepless night of persistent gunfire and bedlam. Fahdi recognized most of the shooting was coming from AK-47s, not M-16s, meaning mostly Iraqi-on-Iraqi gunfire with very little American involvement. The Americans hadn't yet infiltrated the residential neighborhoods; their first mission being to capture and secure the main thoroughfares and strategic arteries of the city. This allowed gangs and pockets of resistance fighters to organize in the shadows of dark alleys and peripheral neighborhoods. Although the U.S. forces had almost everything under control on the surface, thugs were already vandalizing homes and battling each other for control of residential turf right under the Americans' noses.

Fahdi and Marwan had returned to the city unarmed, fearing it could cause them serious headache if they were stopped on the road by any U.S. patrols who may want to search their vehicle. Nonetheless, after that chaotic first night in Baghdad, the first thing Fahdi and his uncle did at Marwan's house the next morning was grab the two AK rifles and several boxes of ammunition Marwan had stored in a closet. They were leery of driving back across town with weapons, but Fahdi's house seemed to be in a calmer area of the city than his uncle's, so they decided to make it their main base. They broke the weapons down into as many pieces as possible and hid the various parts throughout the vehicle.

They spent the next week holed-up there, only leaving to buy food from small, nearby convenience-type stores that were still operating. Inflation in Baghdad grew astronomically as banks continued to be looted and burned in droves across the city, and trade, commerce, and the economy all ground to a dead halt. A single piece of flatbread that cost the equivalent of less than a nickel prior to the invasion now cost a dollar. Many began to fear the city may face dire food shortages before the situation stabilized.

Fahdi's family greatly longed to return home, but conditions in Northern Iraq—security and food wise—were still a lot more stable. He instructed them to remain at the village for a little longer. Kurdistan conducted independent trade with Turkey across Iraq's northern border, meaning Fahdi's family could always cross into Kurdish territory to purchase provisions if food became scarce.

Fortunately, Baghdad did not experience any serious food shortages. Iraq's borders opened wide up (a little too wide in fact) within a couple of weeks of the invasion and imports of all kinds began flowing into the country from Syria, Iran, Turkey, and Jordan. This helped counter the mass inflation and, although the average cost of goods did not fall to pre-war levels, prices came down enough to successfully stabilize Baghdad's economy for the time being.

People who had fled Baghdad began returning home, including Fahdi's family. Security in the residential areas of the city was practically non-existent. Many communities began neighborhood watch-type groups to patrol several square blocks of area and secure it from roving bandits, insurgent groups, and street gangs.

Fahdi's neighborhood was predominantly comprised of Sunni Muslims, many of whom had military, police, and various governmental backgrounds. There were plenty of experienced individuals—Fahdi included—to help organize their local neighborhood watch group and secure their area. Also, considering their former occupations, all were now unequivocally unemployed.

Fahdi's family were the only Christians on the street and the land their house sat on had been passed down to Fahdi's father by his grandfather. The entire region was a large plot of land the Ba'athists broke up and gifted to retiring members of the government in the 1970s. Fahdi's grandfather had worked his way up the ladder to a senior level position within Baghdad's Crime Scene Investigation agency. (For those of you familiar with the popular TV series *C.S.I.*, he was the Iraqi version of Detective Gil Grissom.)

Fahdi's neighborhood watch group, which consisted of about twenty-five men, began securing the area by cordoning off a one-square kilometer section of the neighborhood. Utilizing rocks, bricks, and debris, they erected road blocks to prevent traffic via any peripheral side streets, and established manned checkpoints at the two main entryways into the neighborhood. They then scheduled a rotating watch to ensure each checkpoint was manned by at least two people at all times, while a third two-man team was constantly on patrol to maintain security of the perimeter. No one was allowed in the neighborhood unless they were a resident or personally escorted by a resident. Fahdi later compared it to how the survivors in the hit AMC show *The Walking Dead* would safeguard their settlements.

"It's almost like whoever they have advising the producers for the show on how to establish and maintain security for the neighborhoods must have had experience in Baghdad after the war, because that's exactly how we operated our security teams."

Fahdi and his neighbors were fortunate to get their area secured in a timely manner as the city soon delved into considerable sectarian strife. Shiite Muslim militias banded together and began carrying out revenge killings on Sunni Muslims who had enjoyed special privileges under Saddam's predominantly Sunni regime. With Iraq's border security practically non-existent, Shiite mutineers and radicals flowed in from neighboring Iran, inciting violence and swelling the ranks of the Shiite militias. Suddenly, all the old grudges built up between Iraq's Sunnis and Iran's Shiites during the eight-year Iran-Iraq War of the 1980s were being settled right under the Americans' noses. To counter the Shiite assaults from the East, foreign Sunni extremists flowed into the country from Syria and Jordan on the western side of the country. The two opposing Islamic factions met in the middle of Baghdad in a bloody sectarian brawl that continues more than a dozen years later.

The Americans were caught off guard and found themselves in the middle of a secondary war they didn't expect and were not prepared for. All the U.S. commanders on the ground understood at the time was that Saddam and his cronies were Sunnis, and since the Shiites were enemies of the Sunnis, they must be good. Unfortunately, the enemy of your enemy isn't always your friend. The Shiite militias were heavily influenced and supported by the Iranian government who *did not* have the American's best interests at heart in any way, shape, or form. Essentially, all the U.S. had managed to do was wrest Iraq from the grip of one totalitarian regime and deposit it into the palm of another.

CHAPTER THREE

DOES ANYBODY HERE SPEAK ENGLISH

MAY 2003

It wasn't until late May that American military patrols began penetrating the heart of Baghdad's residential areas. Considering the backgrounds and strong ties to the former Ba'athist regime many of the people in Fahdi's neighborhood had, many of them were extremely nervous at the prospect of U.S. troops knocking on their doors.

"A lot of them believed that after the Americans invaded, they were going to haul us all off to Abu Ghraib."

As word and sightings of American patrols making their way closer and closer to their district emerged, the neighborhood watch group decided to get together to discuss how they would handle the inevitable situation of the Americans rolling into their community.

"We have plenty of weapons and ammo. We should fight and defend our territory," one of the men stated during the meeting.

"Are you insane?" another responded. "The twenty-five of us are going to take on the entire U.S. military?"

"Have you seen the size of their tanks?" Fahdi asked, incredulously.

"There's no way we stand a chance fighting the Americans," one of the men, a former Iraqi Air Force officer, said, taking control of the discussion. His name was Samir and he had been acting as the informal leader of the watch group since its inception. "I recommend we do our best to handle any interaction with the Americans as diplomatically as possible. No matter what, they will have the upper hand. It'll be better for everyone, especially our families, if we do our best to comply."

"When the Americans start raiding this neighborhood, they will arrest most of us. I'd rather go down fighting than be tortured like an animal," a skeptic commented, and several others in the group nodded in agreement.

Samir shook his head and half-laughed at the rampant paranoia floating in the air. "I highly doubt they're torturing anyone. All they wanted was to get rid of Saddam. Trust me, they really don't give a shit about the rest of us."

"At the time, we didn't know being arrested by the Americans meant free food, hot showers, and air conditioned cells, or some of us may have gone willingly."

Mid-morning of the very next day, a U.S. Army convoy of seven Humvees rolled up to the checkpoint of Fahdi's neighborhood. Fahdi was on duty, along with three other guys; all four armed with AK-47s.

Four soldiers emerged from the lead vehicle of the convoy and leveled their M-16s at Fahdi's group. "Please place your weapons on the ground," one of the soldiers shouted in English, then immediately repeated the phrase in extremely broken Arabic. Fahdi and the others reluctantly laid their AKs on the ground. Disarmed and no longer an immediate threat, the Americans lowered their weapons and the same soldier who had commanded them to lay down their AKs motioned for the four Iraqis to approach the convoy. The leader of the unit, a Captain, climbed out of the second Humvee in the line and joined the group.

"Hello, my name is Captain Baker," he said addressing the group in English. "We're here to search the houses of this area for weapons."

Fahdi was the only one in the group who spoke English, and when the Captain said the word "weapons," a couple of the other guys thought he meant WMDs (Weapons of Mass Destruction) and cracked smiles, one even audibly laughed.

"What's so funny?" Captain Baker demanded, obviously not amused.

His harsh tone quickly erased any smiles on the Iraqis' faces and they looked to Fahdi for some indication of what the Captain had said. Fahdi kept his mouth shut and avoided his neighbors' looks, wanting no part in the episode at all.

Captain Baker dropped the issue and motioned to Fahdi's group to push the roadblock to the side of the street, allowing his convoy to move through. They obliged and the soldiers returned to their Humvees. They reassembled the checkpoint and resumed guard as soon as the convoy was through, but did not pick their AKs back up.

As soon as the final vehicle in the convoy cleared the checkpoint, they all stopped and a dozen soldiers exited the Humvees. They broke into two teams of six, approached two neighboring houses and began knocking on the front doors. Knowing the unit had no real translator, Fahdi and one of the other guys decided to abandon the checkpoint and move closer to the Americans, wanting to be able to intervene in a timely manner in case any enmity arose between the troops and their neighbors.

"The soldiers searching the houses immediately started doing shit that wasn't cool. They were patting down the women in the house checking for concealed weapons, rifling through their underwear drawers, and things of that nature. They simply didn't understand what they were doing was improper and exceedingly offensive, but I could feel the frustration and agitation building between the soldiers and the people in the neighborhood with every door they knocked on."

Finally, the tension reached a boiling point.

"You can't do this! You can't touch my wife like that!" Fahdi heard one of his neighbors yelling in Arabic from inside a house.

Shit! Fahdi thought as fear caught in his throat.

By this time, much of the residents on the street were standing out in their yards and heard the man's shouts. Some thought the U.S. soldiers were doing something seriously inappropriate with the women and quickly disappeared back into their homes only to emerge a few seconds later AKs in hand. Fahdi knew the proverbial 'shit was going to hit the fan' unless the situation was neutralized.

"We were probably only a few seconds from a massive firefight with the Americans. And I knew if that happened, we were all dead."

In retrospect, the high implausibility of this being an isolated incident is extremely disheartening. How many other roving units rolled into Baghdad neighborhoods and ended up in bloody shootouts with residents due to simple miscommunications? How many lives were lost in firefights sparked by frustrations stemming from misunderstandings, merely because the U.S. invaded a country and failed to bring along enough people who spoke the native language?

Luckily, Captain Baker made a last-ditch effort to resolve the mounting dispute between his men and the locals diplomatically. "Stand down!" he barked to his two soldiers in a shouting match with Fahdi's neighbor. "Does anyone here speak English?" He yelled, eyeballing the other occupants of the house who were now all seated on the living room floor. Everyone remained silent, but the Captain didn't give up. Fahdi caught sight of him again as he emerged back onto the street. "Does anyone here speak English?!" he screamed again at the top of his lungs. He turned and continued further down the street, shouting the phrase again.

Fahdi took a deep breath and began jogging after the Captain. "Sir," he called out as he caught up to Baker. The Captain spun around on his heels and was noticeably surprised to see Fahdi. "I speak a little English," Fahdi disclosed.

"Why didn't you say something earlier?" Baker asked perturbed.

"I'm sorry, sir, my English isn't very good. I didn't—"

Captain Baker waved his hand visibly irritated. "It'll do," he said abruptly. "Will you help us?" he asked, half-requesting and half-demanding.

"I'll do my best," Fahdi replied.

Fahdi's English was heavily accented and quite broken as he hadn't had much practice conversing with native English speakers. But there was no time to be self-conscious, he just wanted to diffuse the tension in the neighborhood and hoped the Americans would then be on their way. Fahdi and Captain Baker jogged back down the street and returned to the house where the squabble had occurred.

Before going inside, Fahdi explained to Captain Baker why the men in the house had gotten angry with his men. "You can't go in and grab the women and start patting them down and then dig through their underwear drawers," Fahdi said as politely and clearly as possible. "That kind of behavior is going to cause big problems for everyone."

"Well, my first priority is the safety of my men," the Captain retorted. "This is a warzone. Everyone who is not us is a potential enemy and I'm going to take every precaution necessary to ensure these boys return to their families alive."

"I completely understand, sir. I'm just saying, perhaps be a little bit more delicate, that's all."

The Captain grunted but gave a slight nod before marching into the house. "All right everyone," he announced as he and Fahdi entered. "We're all going to relax and discuss things rationally. Do we understand?" Fahdi stepped from behind Baker and translated the Captain's words as closely as possible. And with that, the tension subsided almost immediately and an air of calm settled upon the house.

"Our mission in the neighborhood today is to clear the homes of large or high-powered tactical weapons," Captain Baker declared. "You all can keep your handguns, shotguns, and pistols. You may even keep your AK-47s. What must be turned over to us are any grenades, shoulder-fired missiles, antiaircraft guns, mortars or mortar launchers, landmines, machine guns, and other weapons of this nature."

Fahdi translated the Captain's request. Two of the men seated on the living room floor stood up and responded in Arabic.

"They said they will go to the bedrooms and bring all their weapons here to the living room for you to look at," Fahdi translated for the Captain.

"Do I need to send one of my men to accompany them to the bedrooms?" Captain Baker asked skeptically, his eyes darting between the two men.

Fahdi conveyed the Captain's question in Arabic and the two men timidly shook their heads.

"Go," the Captain instructed. "And tell them to hurry up."

Within a few minutes, a pile of weapons was strewn across the living room floor. Captain Baker's men rummaged through the arms and picked out several items, but left the others on the floor.

"Is this everything?" Captain Baker asked sternly. The men adamantly nodded.

"Ok, we won't go check for ourselves. Please thank them for their cooperation and ask them if they will kindly remain in their home until we have finished searching the rest of the houses on this street." The Captain didn't want one of them running ahead of his team spreading word to other residents the Americans weren't going to search the rooms themselves.

Over the next four hours, Fahdi accompanied the U.S. Army unit to every house in the area within the boundaries the neighborhood watch group had cordoned off. Each interaction played out similarly to how things unfolded at the first house as Fahdi stepped in to translate. The interactions went even more smoothly after Fahdi convinced the U.S. soldiers to civilly knock on the front doors instead of banging with their fists and shouting.

Upon entering, Captain Baker asked for the weapons and the men of the house were typically eager to oblige their requests. The soldiers continued to pat down the male occupants of the houses. Although they did not touch the females, the women were asked to remain seated together in the main room and at least one of the soldiers in the unit never took his eyes off them.

As the unit was returning to their vehicles to load up and head back to their base, the Captain turned to Fahdi. "Where did you learn English?"

"I'm an English Language major at Baghdad University."

"How old are you?"

"Twenty-one."

"Are you a Sunni or Shiite?"

"Neither, I'm Catholic," Fahdi answered. "Remember the house we went in today with all the crucifixes on the walls and the Virgin Mary statues in every room? That was my house."

"Why didn't you say anything?" Captain Baker asked confused.

"I was afraid you'd make me wait outside if you knew it was my house," Fahdi confessed, "and I wanted to make sure that didn't happen."

"Fair enough," the Captain conceded. "How would you like to work for us on a regular basis?"

Unequivocally out of a job and extremely apprehensive about the future of his family's business, Fahdi wanted to scream 'Hell yes!', but didn't want to appear too anxious and simply asked, "Will I get paid?"

The Captain chuckled. "Of course! How about $15 for a full day, and I'll even pay you your entire first month in advance if you show up tomorrow morning."

Fahdi about choked. The average Iraqi salary at the time was equivalent to approximately $6–$10 a month; $15 a day was seriously good money to say the least. "Where and when do I meet you?" he blurted, trying to hide his excitement.

"Be in the parking lot directly outside the main entrance to BIAP (Baghdad International Airport) tomorrow morning at 8 a.m. and I'll find you. What kind of car do you drive?"

"I'll be in a dark blue BMW."

"Oh, you're a rich college boy. You didn't work for Saddam, did you?" The Captain said teasingly, slapping Fahdi on the back.

A flash of panic resonated through Fahdi's body. Grasping

the irony of the moment, that the Captain was sincerely joking, he allowed himself to exhale and the adrenalin rush faded. *Well, define 'worked for,'* he let slip through his consciousness.

The next morning, Fahdi did his best to sneak out of the house without his family noticing. Half-confident Captain Baker would do what he said and give him the job, he didn't want to get his family's hopes up, nor did he really want them (or anyone for that matter) to know about him working for the U.S. military.

Right as Fahdi reached to open the front door, he heard his mom's voice. "Where do you think you are going?"

Busted.

"I'm going to meet a friend," Fahdi lied.

"It's not even 7 a.m. yet. Who are you meeting this early in the morning?" she pressed.

Due to Fahdi's palace security job, his mother knew he had friends who were the sons of high ranking government members in the former regime; some still being sought after by the U.S. military. The last thing she wanted was Fahdi to risk being caught hanging out at his friend's house when the Americans burst through the door to arrest the young man's father, especially considering they usually rounded up everyone in the house and sorted them out later.

Fahdi reassured her he would not go anywhere dangerous. Skeptical, she didn't push the issue any further.

The airport was only about five miles from Fahdi's house. Due to all the checkpoints established by the U.S. forces, slow moving military convoys, and random roadblocks throughout the city, it took Fahdi over an hour to make it through the traffic to the airport, but he got there just in time. Fahdi parked his car but remained inside, scanning the lot for any sign of Captain Baker. The lot was swarming with U.S. troops and vehicles.

Trying to identify one Army Captain was like trying to find a needle in a haystack.

Ten minutes later, there was a knock on Fahdi's passenger side window—Baker.

"I half-expected you not to show," Captain Baker said as Fahdi stepped out of his car.

"Well, I half-expected you not to be here either," Fahdi replied with a smile.

Captain Baker instructed Fahdi to lock his car and then handed him an envelope. Inside were a set of keys and $450 in cash. The Captain then pointed to a small white Nissan car. "You're going to accompany us in that one," he instructed. "It has a full tank of gas. You're good for the day."

"Why can't I take my car?"

"Just do it, and don't ask questions."

Fahdi didn't say another word and got in the Nissan. The Captain instructed him to fall in at the middle of the convoy. The unit traveled to an upper-middle-class neighborhood not far from Fahdi's. They spent the next eight hours going from house to house conducting searches just as they had in Fahdi's neighborhood the day before. Only this time, they *weren't* searching for weapons.

Prior to entering the first house that morning, Captain Baker informed Fahdi their secondary mission was to collect "documents" as well. He didn't elaborate much beyond that and simply told Fahdi to ask the occupants to hand over anything "official looking." From bits and pieces of conversations Fahdi overheard between the soldiers in the unit, he understood it was known numerous high-ranking Ba'ath Party members and government officials resided in the area. The unit was hoping to collect anything to assist the intelligence divisions who were still busy trying to track down Saddam and his sons.

At the end of the day, although the people had willingly handed over stacks and stacks of papers, Fahdi knew it was almost entirely useless drivel.

At the airport parking lot, Fahdi approached the Captain. "Sir, will we be conducting the same type of searches tomorrow?"

"That's the plan," Baker answered, wondering why he wanted to know.

"Look, if you give me an idea of what kind of documents you're looking for, I may be able to help you out a little more. All we collected today is a pile of worthless crap. Some of the papers you boxed up and brought back are literally people's grocery lists."

Captain Baker smiled complacently. "Listen, if you want to continue working with us, I'm going to need you to always do one thing: not ask questions. The only time you should even open your mouth is to translate exactly what I'm saying, when I tell you to say it, and then tell me what they are saying back. You don't ask questions and you certainly do not make suggestions. Is that understood?"

"Yes, sir, I apologize for overstepping," Fahdi replied, but thought, *Suit yourself. As long as you guys keep paying me $450 a month, I'll translate the titles of Disney movies all day long.*

CHAPTER FOUR

ARE YOU TRYING TO GET YOURSELF KILLED?

JUNE-DECEMBER 2003

Fahdi worked as the translator for Captain Baker's unit six days a week from 8 a.m. until 6 p.m. over the next seven months. He met the unit every morning at the airport parking lot and each day they went to a different street or neighborhood in Baghdad and searched the homes for the same things: documents and unauthorized weapons. The Captain always paid Fahdi in advance on the first of every month. He even handed Fahdi another full month's pay of $450 on June 1st even though Fahdi only started working for him towards the end of May and Baker had given him $450 then as well. He told Fahdi to consider the extra money from May a "signing bonus."

After a month with the unit, Baker told Fahdi he could keep the white Nissan to use as his own for the duration of his employment with them. That way he wouldn't have to drive his personal vehicle to the airport and leave it in the lot every day. They also issued him a satellite phone as the unit was beginning to get assigned spontaneous nighttime missions and Baker needed to be able to call Fahdi in to work after hours. Fahdi still had not told anyone, including his own family, about the job with the Americans. After the first week, his mother was extremely suspicious of where her son was disappearing to all day every day, and Fahdi was running out of excuses. All schools throughout Iraq, from primary level through universities, had been on indefinite suspension since the beginning of the war, so he couldn't use college as an excuse.

The evening he returned home driving the Nissan, her suspicions boiled over and she confronted Fahdi as soon as he walked in the front door. "I'm going to ask you one question," she said in an ominous tone as Fahdi walked in the house. "Are you working for the Americans?"

"No," Fahdi lied.

"Are you doing anything illegal?"

"You said one question," he replied curtly and pushed past his mother and continued into the kitchen.

She followed right on his heels. "Then what is going on? Where do you go every morning? Where did the satellite phone come from? And where the hell did you get that car?"

Fahdi assumed a pacifying tone. "Look, the truth is the business isn't doing well," Fahdi explained, referring to the family's veterinary supply company. "We've got to consider other avenues of income. So, my friend and I have been working on building a car import business. Now that the borders are open, there's a fast-growing market for vehicles across the country. The Nissan was one of several cars we bought at one of the bulk auctions Jordanian car dealers are now holding on the border. And since we are having to travel through the middle of nowhere, back and forth between the border, we needed satellite phones. We've already sold a couple of cars, which is where the money we are currently living on comes from."

The part about the family business struggling was the honest truth. Since the beginning of the war, electricity in Baghdad, and across the entire country for that matter, was, to put it mildly, sporadic. At best, they had two or three hours of power a day. Generators became a highly-coveted item and their value skyrocketed. A good deal of the business's profit was made by selling antibiotics, but many of them needed to be refrigerated. In order to generate enough power to consistently refrigerate the amount of antibiotics and other medicines the business needed to maintain in order to remain profitable, they desperately needed a generator, several in fact. Fahdi calculated the cost for the generators would run approximately $30,000, and although his family had been relatively affluent prior to the war, they didn't have half that amount saved up.

Fahdi's mom was not sure of his truthfulness, but she decided not to ask any more questions. "Please promise me you won't do anything to put yourself or anyone else in this family in danger," she asked solemnly.

Fahdi nodded with a lump in his throat. He wanted to do what was best for his country and, above all, his family, but his gut told him the path he'd chosen was a treacherous one.

As Captain Baker and his unit's searches pushed deeper into less "reputable" portions of Baghdad and the initial adoration many Iraqis had for their U.S. "liberators" transformed into resentment toward the American "occupiers," Fahdi began to regret convincing Captain Baker to conduct his weapons searches in such a placid manner. His soldiers continued to simply knock on doors and ask residents to surrender any weapons larger than an AK-47, and sometimes weren't even entering houses anymore and would politely wait on the front porch as the occupants brought out the requested items. Word of these methods spread like wildfire across Baghdad. The Americans essentially disarmed law-abiding citizens who trusted and supported them, while those who harbored malicious feelings and intent toward the U.S. forces retained their weapons, simply stashing them out of sight until the Americans moved on to the next house.

After seeing this occur over the course of several weeks, Fahdi could no longer keep his mouth shut. He approached the Captain one evening after they had returned to the airport at the end of a long day of searches and seizures. "Sir, I know you asked me to keep my mouth shut and not give you advice on how to do your job, but do you realize over the past couple of weeks all we've done is take weapons away from good people and allow bad ones to keep theirs? And, as I'm sure you've noticed, animosity throughout this city is only growing for you and the rest of the Americans. I have a bad feeling, as you say, 'shit is going to hit the fan' real soon."

"Fahdi, you're absolutely right," Baker replied, shocking Fahdi with his nonchalant response, but Fahdi felt in his gut there was more to it than that. "And when the 'shit hits the fan,' how are we going to identify who the 'bad guys' are?"

Fahdi had no response and simply shrugged.

"Will they be wearing uniforms?" Baker asked. "Will they have stickers on their shirts saying, 'Hi, my name is Insurgent'?"

"No, of course not," Fahdi answered sheepishly. "No, they're going to look just like you or any other citizen of this city, but we're going to have a good idea of who they are," Baker said as he climbed back into his Humvee and slammed the door. "They'll be the ones carrying the unauthorized weapons."

Fahdi wasn't sure if this had been a premeditated strategy or if the Captain was simply doing his best to see the bright side of an extremely dangerous situation the Americans were getting themselves into. Regrettably, the latter was closer to reality.

By the Fall of 2003, the citizens of Iraq desperately wanted some normalcy to return to their lives. A small step in that direction came the day the schools reopened nationwide. Since the previous school year had been cut short by about two months and the current school year was already off to a late start, the Iraqi Ministry of Education administered standardized tests to all students to determine if they should remain at the same grade level they had begun the previous school year at or if they would be allowed to promote on to the next level. Both Fahdi's brother and sister passed their tests. Fareed began his senior year of high school and Farrah entered 9th grade. To commemorate her children's academic achievements, Fahdi's mom invited a few family members and close friends to the house for a small soiree.

While everyone was gathered in the living room enjoying tea, the husband of one of Fahdi's mother's friends turned to Fahdi. "Hey, I thought I saw you driving in the middle of an America convoy the other day, like you were going somewhere with them. Are you working with the Americans now?"

Fahdi did his best to feign obliviousness. "No, it wasn't me," he said coolly and shifted his eyes to his mother who sat silently sipping her tea.

"Hmm, it sure looked a lot like you," the man persisted. "But you weren't driving your car, you were in a white Nissan."

To help convince his mom he and his friend were in fact working on building a car dealership, around the end of the summer, Fahdi had told her he'd sold the Nissan through the business. The truth was he'd simply stopped driving it home and had been parking it at a friend's house. He'd go every morning before work to switch it out with his BMW and return each evening to park it for the night.

Not knowing Fahdi's working relationship with the Americans, his friend was very happy with the arrangement. He didn't have a car of his own and Fahdi told him he could use the BMW anytime he wanted while it was parked at his house.

As soon as the bigmouth mentioned the white Nissan, Fahdi's heart sank. His mom continued to silently sip her tea, but Fahdi clearly watched as an icy glaze appeared in her eyes. In an instant, he knew that she knew.

One cold morning in January 2004, Fahdi was waiting in the airport parking lot to meet up with Captain Baker and his unit to start their usual workday. When the Captain arrived, Fahdi could tell by the look on his face something was wrong.

"You're not going to be able to work with us today," Baker said in a solemn tone as he approached Fahdi. "Actually, I technically have to fire you today."

"What? Why?" Fahdi asked frantically. "Did I do something wrong?"

"No, not at all," the Captain replied, consolingly putting a hand on Fahdi's shoulder. "You're an excellent translator and you've done a great job with us. You wouldn't be here if it were an issue with your job performance. Orders have come from the top that we are no longer allowed to informally employ locals as translators. There is a new company, called Titan, operating out of the Green Zone now, that oversees all hiring and management of translators for the U.S. forces. You're going to have to formally apply and be hired by them to continue working as a translator. If you manage to land a position with the company,

I'll do my best to make sure you get assigned back to our unit, but I can't keep you on or continue to pay you without you being officially employed by Titan. I'm sorry."

"Okay, I understand," Fahdi said, calming down a little now that there was hope he could retain his job. "Where do I need to go to apply?"

"Ride with us," the Captain said motioning for Fahdi to get in the back of his Humvee. "We'll get you into the Green Zone and drop you at Titan's headquarters. Then you're on your own to land the job."

As their Humvee pulled up in front of a row of several pre-fab work trailers just inside the Green Zone, Fahdi noticed a group of a few dozen other locals crowded near the entrance to the trailer with a makeshift sign hanging on the door: TITAN HQ.

"They will open at 9 a.m. to start the screenings," Captain Baker explained as Fahdi exited the Humvee. "Also, I'm going to need the keys to the Nissan and the Satellite phone I issued you." Fahdi handed over the requested items. "If things go well, you'll be here most of the day. I hear their hiring process is 'thorough.' Are you going to be able to get a ride home from here?"

Fahdi nodded.

"Don't look so glum kid. I'm sure you'll be hired and we'll be seeing you in a couple of days," Baker said with a smile before driving off.

Fahdi walked over and joined the group of other locals waiting outside the trailer. No one spoke a word and everyone had a forlorn look on their face. Most likely, they had gotten the same disheartening news from the units they were working with. When they awoke that morning, they had steady, good-paying jobs in a city burning to the ground around them. Now, they'd all had the rug pulled out from underneath them, tossing their livelihood and futures to the wind.

Promptly at 9 a.m., the door to the trailer opened and an American Titan employee stepped out and addressed the group in Arabic. It was the first time Fahdi had heard an American speaking Arabic. Two other workers appeared and started passing out clipboards with paperwork to everyone in the group.

The candidates were instructed to fill out the "applications" in English, which asked basic demographic questions: name, date of birth, religious affiliation, etc. Obviously, the company wasn't bound by any sort of Equal Opportunity Employment laws. As the translators handed in their completed paperwork, they were called into the trailer to take a language test to assess their English fluency levels. Fahdi felt confident in his English skills now, having worked nearly every day with Captain Baker's unit for the past eight months, and easily passed the exam. Several of his fellow applicants, however, were not as fortunate; about a dozen failed the language test and were asked to leave but were told they could reapply in a month.

Those who passed the exam, including Fahdi, were told to report to the trailer next door to undergo the next stage of the hiring process, a "security screening." Inside the security trailer, the candidates were given another large packet of paperwork to fill out with forms asking various background questions and instructions to not only list the names of their immediate family members, but to map out their family tree including first through third cousins. For Iraqis, who typically have quite large families, this was a massive list of names for most of the applicants. Once the background forms were complete, each candidate underwent a one-on-one interview with a Titan hiring manager in a small, windowless room. To Fahdi it felt more like an interrogation. Even the first words out of his interviewer's mouth were, "Try not to think of this as an interrogation," as Fahdi took a seat on a small metal folding chair. "Consider it a friendly chat between two pals at a coffee shop," the man added with a fake smile.

The interview lasted about an hour. Fahdi was asked numerous questions about his background while the interviewer scribbled notes on a yellow legal pad. Fahdi was terrified he'd be asked a question forcing him to disclose his previous job as a Palace security guard, but nothing requiring him to specifically declare this ever came up, and he sure wasn't going to offer that info up willingly. "Were you in the Iraqi Army?" the interviewer asked Fahdi.

"No, I was in college before the war."

"Would you have joined the Army after college?"

"Well, military service in Iraq is mandatory."

"Were you in the Ba'ath Party?"

"Yes. Everyone was technically in the Ba'ath Party." Fahdi was a little confused, not sure if these were trick questions or if the Americans were really this clueless about Iraq.

"Tell me about your father."

"My father is dead. He died when I was ten."

"You do know we will be verifying everything you say in here today," the interviewer said in a cautionary tone.

"Go for it," Fahdi replied casually.

"Who raised you and your siblings?"

"My mom and her brothers."

"Were any of your uncles in the Army?"

"Yes, all of them. They all fought in the Iran-Iraq War. One died and one is still classified as 'Missing-in-Action,' but we're sure he is dead, too. Two of my uncles also fought in Desert Storm."

"What do you think of Saddam?"

Fahdi shrugged, "Honestly, nothing really."

"Do you hate him?"

Fahdi shook his head. "No."

"So, you supported Saddam?"

"No."

"Well, you either like him or you don't, which is it?"

"I didn't know the guy. He didn't do anything to help or hurt me. I really have no opinion. To me, he was just the President. He never killed anyone in my family and he never stopped by my house to hand me money. No love and no grudge."

"You realize he killed a lot of innocent people, right?"

"All I know is he was the President and it wasn't my business or place to question him. I made sure to never do anything against his policies or piss him off, and he was very clear on what would get you into trouble."

"What do you think of the Americans being here?"

"So far so good," Fahdi replied. "For the first time, people can say what they want without having to worry about someone reporting it to the government and having them come kill you or your family."

"So, I'm guessing you'd consider this an improvement?" the interviewer asked with a hint of sarcasm.

"Sure."

Fahdi wasn't feeling too confident about the interview up to that point, but then he launched his silver bullet: his religion.

"Are you Sunni or Shiite?"

"Neither, I'm Christian."

"Oh, well, that's unique." The man was generally surprised and immediately dropped his suspicious tone and cheerily said, "Well, I think we have all we need. Go have a seat in the waiting room while we finish up the other interviews and review our notes."

Fahdi returned to the waiting room of the Security Screening trailer where he sat for the next five hours. Finally, late in the afternoon, a new Titan official, none of the translators had seen before, showed up and addressed the group. "If I call your name, please step outside."

"We didn't know whether to hope our name was called or not. He didn't clarify if calling our name meant we were hired, disqualified, perhaps going to prison, or what. But since those whose names were called were told to go outside, we assumed it was a bad sign."

Out of the twenty-five translators who had made it to the interview stage and were now in the waiting room, the Titan official called out only six of their names. Fahdi's was one of them. Outside, the "chosen six" assumed they were being sent home.

The official emerged from the Security Screening trailer and told them to follow him over to the third and final trailer in the Titan group. Closing the door, he turned to the group and said, "Congratulations. We'd like to offer the six of you positions as local translators with the Titan Corporation."

Fahdi was genuinely surprised. *If I got hired, what-the-hell did those other guys say in the interview?* He'd spent the last five hours going over every question he'd been asked and scrutinizing all his answers. He kicked himself for not saying more "pro U.S." things and worried he should have more passionately espoused dislike for Saddam. However, when all was said and done, these types of answers were exactly what got the other applicants disqualified. The Titan interviewers knew full well everyone was technically in the Ba'ath Party. Subsequently, anyone who vehemently denied any part in it was immediately red flagged. They also knew full well all males in Iraq were required to serve in the military. Those who said they were never in the military and would have never gone into the military were either lying or had special privileges granted by the government to sidestep their military service. Either way, red flag.

The six new hires were taken for fingerprinting and photos and issued official Titan employee badges granting them access to the Green Zone and the airport. After assignment to their specific units, they would receive additional credentials allowing them entrance onto the base and into any other restricted areas their unit would need them to have access to. New badges in hand, they were instructed to return to Titan HQ the next morning to receive their unit assignments.

"Welcome to Titan. Good luck and be safe," the Titan official said in a welcoming tone before dismissing the new linguists for the day, then added more sternly, "Don't show your badge to anyone or give it to anyone. And again, congratulations."

Fahdi was elated and couldn't wait to get back to work with Captain Baker and his unit.

The following morning, Fahdi and the five other translators from the group who'd been hired reported back to Titan HQ in the Green Zone at 9 a.m. This time they were greeted by a female U.S. Army Sergeant who approached the six translators with a clipboard and told each of them what unit they had been assigned to work for. "Sameer—42nd Infantry Division; Rami—82nd Airborne, Fahdi—2nd Infantry Division . . ."

Of course, the names of these units may as well have been in Ancient Greek because neither Fahdi nor any of the other translators had the slightest idea what they meant. Fahdi simply assumed "2nd Infantry Division" must be the official name of Captain Baker's unit, then the Sergeant dropped the bomb.

"All of you will be remaining here in Baghdad, except you," she said spinning on her heels to face Fahdi.

"You will be shipping out tomorrow to meet up with your unit in Ramadi."

Fahdi's stomach sank. *Did she say Ramadi?*

She handed each translator a paper with pertinent information and points of contact regarding their assigned units: where the units were located, what base they were assigned to, the unit commander, who the translator's point of contact would be within the unit, etc. Fahdi stared at his paper in disbelief.

2ND INFANTRY DIVISION RAMADI, AL-ANBAR, IRAQ
CAMP AR-RAMADI
UNIT COMMANDER: CPT. TIMOTHY ROWE

"There must be some mistake," Fahdi blurted with a twinge of panic in his voice. "I already work with a unit. I work for Captain Baker, here in Baghdad. I've been with him for eight months. He's expecting me. Here's the number to his satellite phone. Call him." Fahdi quickly jotted down Captain Baker's number on the back of his unit assignment and thrust it toward the female Sergeant.

"We actually spoke with Captain Baker this morning," she replied ignoring Fahdi's paper. "He called here asking about you. We told him you had, in fact, been hired on but you were needed more in Ramadi. He understood and said to tell you it was a pleasure working with you and good luck out west."

Fahdi only half-believed she'd talked to Captain Baker. He had a gut feeling Baker was clueless about the whole situation. "Well, I'm not going to Ramadi. If I can't work here in Baghdad I'm quitting," Fahdi declared matter-of-factly.

"Did we mention it's more money?" the Sergeant replied cannily. "You'll make $600 a month. We're short on linguists out there and are really hoping you'll accept the position. You'll be one of the first locals assigned to that unit, which is why we are offering the pay incentive."

The mention of the increase in pay did give Fahdi cause to

reconsider, but it did not cinch the deal. "Driving to and from Ramadi every day is suicidal. It's not worth $600," he finally said after mulling it over.

The Sergeant smiled. "You won't be commuting. You'll live on base with the American soldiers and be free to come home on the weekends if you like. You'll have your own sleeping quarters on the base, enjoy free meals at the chow hall, and have access to the PX. Do me a favor and give it a try. You can quit at any time, but at least give it two weeks."

Fahdi wasn't sure what a 'chow hall' was, but clearly understood "free meals," and his curiosity urged him to learn more about this "PX" place. He also thought it would be kind of cool to see what it's like to live as an American soldier for a little while. He finally conceded. "I guess I'll see you tomorrow, Sergeant."

Shipping off to Ramadi was only part of the issue. What worried Fahdi even more than heading for what was quickly shaping up to be the very bloody front lines of the war was the fact he'd now have to come clean to his mom. There was no way he'd be able to keep up the ruse of him and his buddy running a car import business under these circumstances.

"I knew it! All these months you've been lying to me," his mom spat after Fahdi apprised her of the truth that he'd been working for the Americans. "We don't even know what their endgame is! I don't trust them and you shouldn't either. *Just stay out of it!*"

"It's good money! And in case you haven't noticed, our options for making a living are extremely limited right now." Then he dropped the bomb about shipping off to Ramadi.

"Are you trying to get yourself killed?"

"So far it's been safe. Nothing even remotely dangerous has happened around me. I'm not fighting. I'm not carrying a gun. All I do is talk. It's no big deal. And I honestly enjoy doing it."

"Please, Fahdi, don't go. I don't want you to go," she begged, holding his hands in hers.

"I have to. We need the money. The business is dead and I don't want Fareed to have to drop out of school and go to work. We really don't have a choice. I'm going."

CHAPTER FIVE

HEADED FOR THE FRONT LINES

JANUARY 2004

The next morning Fahdi's brother dropped him off at the Green Zone entrance closest to the Titan trailers.

In addition to Fahdi, there were two other translators shipping out to Ramadi who were already waiting in the main Titan trailer as Fahdi walked in. Unlike Fahdi, they were Iraqi nationals who flew in from the U.S. and hadn't lived in Iraq for nearly twenty years. They'd been recruited by Titan stateside, who was offering annual salaries of over $120K to Iraqis with U.S. citizenship or permanent residency. Many Iraqis and other native Arabic speakers, who oftentimes were working minimum wage jobs in the U.S., quickly jumped at the opportunity to make the same salary as some surgeons. But more often than not, they found themselves in the middle of hell dodging mortars in a Fallujah ditch and quickly realized $120,000 a year wasn't nearly enough and were on the next flight back to the U.S.

Fahdi and the other translators waited almost all day at the Titan trailer for a driver to arrive and take them to Ramadi. Finally, at 4 p.m., an American Titan employee pulled up in a four-door, Nissan pickup truck and told the group he was their ride to Ramadi. The four occupants spent the duration of the two-hour drive from Baghdad to Ramadi in complete silence.

Upon arrival at Camp Ramadi, the three translators were issued additional badges granting them access on and off of the base. With those in hand, two Army Sergeants showed up to escort them to their living quarters and give them a quick tour of the camp.

One Sergeant took charge of the men from the U.S., while the other, Sergeant Ryan, introduced himself as Fahdi's escort. It was the last time Fahdi saw the two translators from Baghdad.

Fahdi and Sergeant Ryan's first stop was the large garrison Fahdi would call home for the next few days. The long narrow building was lined on both sides with green military cots. Fahdi estimated the room could sleep approximately eighty.

So much for my own room.

Since it was after 7 p.m., the barracks were swarming with American soldiers performing their nightly routines: showering, socializing, trading snacks they swiped from the chow hall at dinner, etc.

For Fahdi, it was a bit of a culture shock, considering it was the first time he'd observed U.S. military members during their "off duty" hours. The stony glares, precision actions, systematic movements, crisp uniforms, and brusque dialogue Fahdi was accustomed to seeing from soldiers in full gear patrolling the streets of Baghdad had suddenly transformed into boisterous banter and continuous practical jokes between a bunch of young guys in nylon shorts and flip flops. Fahdi felt as if all eighty pairs of eyes were trained on him alone as he and Ryan snaked their way through the horde to the single empty cot at the very back of the room.

"They're all looking at me funny," Fahdi whispered to Ryan as he set his small bag of belongings on the cot.

"Well, you're probably going to be working with a lot of these guys. I suggest you start making friends ASAP."

Sergeant Ryan then showed Fahdi around and did his best to indoctrinate Fahdi into U.S. military life in forty-five minutes. He taught him a few key Army terms—latrine, chow hall, PX, barracks, etc.—and showed him where everything was located, including the gym and rec room complete with TVs, computers, and Xbox and PlayStation videogame consoles. *Maybe this place won't be so bad after all.*

After his brief indoctrination, Ryan took Fahdi for his first meal in the military chow hall.

"It was like paradise. It reminded me of a movie I'd seen as a kid, *Charlotte's Web*; specifically, the scene where the rat was roaming around the fairgrounds at night singing and eating everything. That was totally me during my first chow hall visit."

The far wall of the chow hall was lined with glass front convenience store coolers stocked to the brim with a variety of canned beverages—Red Bull, Gatorade, Starbucks iced cappuccinos, every brand and flavor of soda under the sun; freezers full of single-serve ice cream and other desserts; a full salad bar and hot entrée line with servers dishing out steaks, pork chops, cheeseburgers, and more.

"So, what am I allowed to eat?" Fahdi asked Ryan after surveying the facility.

"Anything you want, man."

"Well, how much are we allowed to take?"

"As much as you can eat, while you're in here. They don't like food being taken back to the barracks. But all the guys sneak ice creams and Red Bulls back and no one gives 'em any shit about it."

"No wonder you guys kicked the Iraqi Army's ass, look at what they feed you! Iraqi soldiers get flat bread and water, and only if it's a really special occasion, they may get to smell some chicken. Then they're told, 'Now go fight. And you better fucking win!'"

Fahdi ate too much that first evening in Ramadi and very much regretted it later.

After dinner, Ryan took Fahdi for another thrilling experience, his first trip to the base PX. He was like a kid in a candy store.

"I blew about fifty bucks on crap," Fahdi reminisced later. "But at the time, a lot of it was unique stuff I'd never really seen before: a Swiss Army knife, a military flashlight with different colored filters, American-style sunglasses, magazines, and a bunch of other stuff I don't even remember now."

Ryan dropped Fahdi back off at the barracks and told him to get some sleep; that he'd be back in the morning to take him to meet Captain Rowe, the Army officer Fahdi would be working for.

Before turning in for the night, Fahdi desperately craved one more pleasure . . . a good shower. He dug his toothbrush and a change of clothes out of his small rucksack and headed for the shower trailer and was surprised to discover he needed to provide his own toiletries.

"After seeing all the five-star amenities throughout the camp, I figured there would be an attendant at the showers squirting high-dollar shampoo into the soldiers' hands while they bathed. You'd think Ryan would have suggested I buy some soap at the PX instead of a bunch of stocking-stuffers."

He gave himself a thorough rinsing and brushed his teeth

with water, then returned to his cot and tinkered with his new "toys" until the wee hours of the morning.

At 9 a.m. the next morning, Fahdi groggily opened his eyes to see Sergeant Ryan's face staring down at him. "Good morning princess," Ryan said teasingly. "You wanna put some pants on so we can go meet Captain Rowe?"

"Can we get some food first, I'm starving."

"Hate to rain on your parade, but you totally missed breakfast, dude," Ryan replied shoving Fahdi's shoes towards him.

"Seriously? Why didn't you come get me sooner?"

"I did! You were dead to the world at 6 a.m."

"Oh shit, never mind. Why does everything have to start in the middle of the night with you people?"

"They'll start serving lunch in a couple of hours. Can you make it until then or do you want to stop by the PX to grab a snack on our way to meet Captain Rowe?"

"No, I'll be fine. Let's go meet the Captain."

Ryan and Fahdi made their way to a makeshift office building on the far side of the camp; basically, four large Conex trailers that had all been pushed together, connected via plywood breezeways, and then divvied up into different office spaces. A large chain length fence with razor wire ran behind the trailers, marking the edge of the American camp, but Fahdi noticed it appeared to be more of a "military camp" on the other side of the fence. The gate between the two sides was not far and was heavily guarded.

Fahdi wanted to ask Ryan what the story was behind the razor wire fence separating the two sides of the camp, but had a feeling meeting Captain Rowe would answer any questions.

He was right.

They entered the first trailer and turned right into the first office. Fahdi was surprised by how nice the insides of the trailers were. The office was furnished with a large, solid wood executive desk, plush leather chairs, a small couch, and several other furnishings. Standing behind the desk talking on the phone was Captain Rowe.

"Yes sir, we're going to get the next group going tomorrow," Captain Rowe said into the phone. "Roger that, sir. If it's no trouble, can I call you back after chow? I think my translator is finally here . . . . Ok, great."

Rowe hung up the phone and stared at Fahdi and Ryan for a few uncomfortable seconds. In his early thirties, he appeared to Fahdi to be half African-American and half Asian. Extremely fit, he was most intimidating.

"So, you're my translator," Rowe finally broke the silence. "I hear you like your beauty sleep," he said disdainfully stepping from behind the desk and moving closer to Fahdi and Ryan.

Fahdi kept his mouth shut.

"I'm Captain Rowe, and although you won't be working directly with me, I'll be your immediate supervisor and you'll report to me."

Fahdi nodded.

"You're going to be translating for the U.S. Army drill sergeants who are training the new ICDC recruits."

ICDC (Iraqi Civil Defense Corp) was the new Iraqi Army the U.S. was building back up after disbanding the old Army under Saddam.

"The training will be conducted on the Iraqi side of the base, which I'm sure you noticed on your way in, right next door." Rowe paused for reaction. "There are 150 new trainees starting basic training tomorrow, then another 150 will start right after this group graduates. I need a company of 194. Hopefully, there will be that many left of the 300 once Sergeant Benning is done with them. They will be the very first company from

Al Anbar province to enter the ICDC basic training program and they need to be ready to fight alongside US Marines in a matter of weeks.

"We've got seven drill sergeants and, as of now, one translator—you. We requested two more terps (interpreters) but they haven't gotten here yet. We are hoping you'll get some backup soon. The head drill instructor is Sergeant Benning. Ryan will take you over to their tent after lunch to meet him so you'll at least know who to look for tomorrow morning. You'll meet with the Sergeants every morning at their tent and ride over to the Iraqi side of the base. After you've been relieved in the afternoon, you're free for the remainder of the day, except on Fridays. Every Friday afternoon, you are to report here for a weekly meeting.

"If you have any problems, questions, concerns, anything at any point, you come to me. You don't ask the drill sergeants questions or go to them with any issues, you come to me. Do you have any questions?"

Fahdi had a million questions running through his mind but didn't even know where to begin. He just shook his head and said, "No, sir."

From Captain Rowe's office Ryan took Fahdi to the tent where the drill sergeants stayed, and introduced him to Sergeant Benning, a tall, slender, African-American in his mid-thirties. As Fahdi describes him, a tough mother fucker.

Aside from Benning, there were six other drill sergeants, but the one who captivated Fahdi immediately was Sgt. Martinez.

"His biceps were as big around as my head and he had the most amazing tattoo I've ever seen. It was a picture of a woman who looked like she was standing when he had his arm straight, and like she was sitting when he bent his arm. I used to love to work out with him just to watch the tattoo during bench presses," Fahdi said with a smile, taking a drag from his cigarette.

Sgt. Benning barely gave Fahdi a second glance as Ryan introduced them. "Nice to meet you. Be here at zero six hundred tomorrow," Benning said briskly without even looking up from some paperwork he was looking over.

Fahdi, not yet familiar with military time format and clueless as to what zero six hundred meant said, "Roger that, Sergeant. I'll be here. Just one question, what is zero six hundred?"

Benning slowly looked up and starred at Fahdi straight faced. He could not believe his ears. "Zero . . . six . . . hundred," Benning repeated more forcefully.

"I-I'm sorry, I've just never heard this before," Fahdi stammered.

"They've sent me an idiot," Benning said looking at Ryan. "Do you even speak English?" He cut his eyes back to Fahdi.

"I've been talking to you, haven't I?" Fahdi replied somewhat cockily.

"Great, and you're a smart ass, too." Benning had clearly lost his patience.

Before Fahdi could respond, Ryan jumped in. "We better go. I have to get Fahdi over to HQ for some more in-processing," he said, practically shoving Fahdi out of the tent.

On the return walk, Ryan taught Fahdi military time. Considering he would have to report early the next morning, Fahdi realized he'd have to find his way back to Sergeant Benning's tent in the pitch dark. He relayed this fear to Ryan who offered to walk Fahdi to Benning's tent and back that evening by flashlight. Later in the week, Ryan also arranged to have Fahdi move to a barracks tent closer to Benning's.

The next morning, Fahdi made a couple of wrong turns on his way to meet Benning and the other drill sergeants, arriving about ten minutes late. By the time he showed up, Benning and the others were all loaded up in the Humvee waiting for Fahdi.

Benning eyeballed Fahdi distastefully and said in an icy tone, "Get in," but didn't comment on his tardiness.

Once on the Iraqi side of the base, Benning broke the tense silence. "What time did I tell you to be at our tent this morning?" Benning asked Fahdi in a patronizing tone.

"Six o'clock," Fahdi responded coolly.

"What time did you show up?"

"About six o'clock."

"Actually, it was 6:11, to be exact."

"Okay?"

"No, *not* 'okay'!" Benning replied raising his voice. "Next time I say '0600,' your ass better be here at 0545! Or, better yet, be here at 0530 because I just *might* want to leave a little early!"

"Well why didn't you just tell me you wanted me at 5:45 yesterday?"

"*Oh, my God!* Are you still talking to me? You better be there at 0530 tomorrow morning. If you're one minute late, I will make you come at 0400 the next morning. You will then come an hour earlier the following morning for every day you are late. I'll make your ass show up the night before and wait outside my tent until it's time to leave in the morning if you push me, you little fuck!"

Fahdi finally took a hint and shut his mouth.

Benning gunned the Humvee and steered between two tents serving as the drill instructors offices on the ICDC training base and slammed on the brakes. Benning and the other drill sergeants piled out of the vehicle and Fahdi followed them into the larger of the two tents.

"The recruits are supposed to be here and ready to start training at 9 a.m.," Benning shared with Fahdi as they entered the office. "But if I've learned anything about Iraqis, it's they aren't the most punctual of people," he paused and eyeballed Fahdi. "I don't expect we'll get any training underway until around ten or there 'bouts."

Open registration to join the new Iraqi Army had been underway for several weeks and was open to any males between the ages of eighteen and forty for enlisted members, while those who had served as officers in the former Iraqi Army could be of any age to rejoin the new Army being formed under the eye of the U.S. Regardless, they were still required to attend boot camp alongside the new recruits—farmers, shop owners, students, etc.—fresh off the street. The driving force behind the volunteers was pure, hard cash. The pay was $60 a month in regular salary and an additional $80 a month in hazard pay. This was decent money by Baghdad standards and extremely good pay for rural areas like Ramadi, particularly in the wake of the war which left the economy in shambles and skyrocketing unemployment. The most significant challenge Sgt. Benning and his drill instructors faced was cramming three months of basic training into three weeks and battling a language barrier every step of the way.

At approximately 8 a.m., the phone in the Drill Instructor's office rang. Benning answered. Fahdi recognized Captain Rowe's bellowing voice coming through the receiver, though he couldn't make out what the Captain was saying.

"Roger that, sir. I'll send one of my guys over to pick them up now," Benning replied into the phone. "Looks like you've got some back-up," Benning said to Fahdi as he hung up. "Two more terps just showed up from Baghdad and are in the Captain's office waiting for a ride." Benning told one of his guys to run over with the Humvee and pick up the new translators and bring them back.

Benning briefed the three terps on their roles and responsibilities during the upcoming training. "Say everything we say, when we say it, and how we say it," Benning instructed, "and don't fuck up. We will be using military terminology. If you don't know the meaning of something, ask for clarification. If the recruits do something wrong, I'm not going to assume you screwed up, I am going to assume they are fuck ups and they will be punished. Bottom line: everything the drill sergeants say must be translated exactly as we say it—same tone and everything. If we're upset, you're upset. If we're happy, you're happy. If we are screaming, your ass better be screaming, too. You got it?"

The toughest part for Fahdi was translating all the profanity. "We did a lot of screaming, most of which was cussing. The drill sergeants were screaming for no reason, all the time. It's really hard to translate a sentence containing eight 'fucks' a couple of 'assholes' and perhaps two words with any meaning.

The terps also found it difficult to convey the proper emotion toward the recruits Benning required. When he screamed in someone's face, he expected the translators to get up in the recruit's face and yell, too. Fahdi found it very awkward having to scream in the face of a complete stranger who had done nothing to personally anger him.

"I learned to be a really good actor because if I wasn't screaming at the trainees, Benning was screaming at me, and that guy scared the shit out of me. I made sure to do everything I had to in order to keep him happy."

Just as Benning had predicted, the bulk of the new recruits didn't show up until nearly 10 a.m. They had been instructed to wear "workout clothing" for the first day of training and then, if they made it through the first day, they'd be fitted for official uniforms. By 10:30 a.m., there were nearly 150 trainees lined up in the training yard. Predictably, some of Rowe's 150 selectees had gotten cold feet before even starting. They were a riff-raff group of Iraqi males mostly dressed in Adidas track suits.

The first day of training was simply, as Benning described to Fahdi, a mission to "separate the men from the boys." For the first two hours, Benning and his men conducted a hard-core, non-stop PT (Physical Training) session to "warm up" the recruits.

"They had them running, jumping, doing push-ups, and jumping jacks, low crawling, and all kinds of stuff to break them down and weed-out the quitters. And if anyone started to slow down or looked like they were getting tired, a drill sergeant screamed in their face. I don't even know how they did it, but somehow eight drill sergeants were literally on top of almost 150 guys. Not one recruit was able to slack off for more than a few seconds before Benning or one of his guys was on top of him, barking in his face about what a piece of shit he was."

Not only were the recruits being "whipped into shape," but the translators were as well. They had best keep up with the drill sergeants and constantly be ready to scream at and harass the recruits right alongside them.

At one point, Benning climbed to the top of one of the massive hills of dirt and sand the base construction crews had bulldozed together to form a makeshift barrier between the Iraqi and U.S. side of the base. Fahdi stuck with him like glue as he ordered the trainees, now soaked in sweat, to repeatedly run up the hill and roll down to the bottom. Recruits would make it to the top and Benning would randomly push some of them back down, chuckling as they rolled uncontrollably to the bottom. He even instructed Fahdi to do the same.

A dozen recruits washed out within the first half hour of training; some quit on their own; others drill sergeants sent home. If a recruit complained about being tired and sat down to rest, he was out. If they sustained an injury that kept them from running, they were out. Anyone who washed out was given the opportunity to reapply but had to wait two weeks and start the process from the very beginning. By the end of the day, forty-one recruits had quit or been kicked out by Benning's team.

Later that day, Fahdi overheard Captain Rowe ask Benning to tone it down a little as they were already below the number of recruits expected to graduate from the first class. "I personally think you are doing a fantastic job and support you 100%, but at this point, it's quantity over quality." Ostensibly, Rowe simply needed warm bodies to fill uniforms.

CHAPTER SIX

BOOT CAMP

FEBRUARY 2004

Fahdi wasn't only on time to meet Benning and the other drill sergeants the second morning of training, he was a half hour early. The last thing he wanted was Benning in his face again. The recruits who had survived the previous day's "qualification round" of boot camp were instructed to arrive at zero-six-thirty for the remainder of their training. Most were late. Needless to say, Benning ensured they were properly punished, but did not push any of them to the breaking point in order to uphold Captain Rowe's request.

Satisfied all the tardy recruits had been properly reprimanded, Benning ordered everyone to line up to receive their official training uniforms: a long-sleeved brown jumpsuit, a pair of black combat boots, a canteen, and a web belt.

"Those jump suits looked hot as hell. I really felt bad for the recruits having to wear them and run around in the heat. And the boots looked old and crappy. It was all probably shit the U.S. had left over from Vietnam."

The trainees were instructed to wear a white t-shirt under their jumpsuits and to wear them every day of the training. Upon successful completion of the program, they'd be issued official ICDC dessert camouflage uniforms.

After everyone had changed, the drill sergeants had the recruits line up in formation and Benning addressed the group.

"This course is not only about physical training," Benning announced as Fahdi translated. "In addition to PT, you will also be given classroom instruction on various topics. Today you will learn about military structure, hierarchy, and terminology as well as the basics of democracy. But first, you will decide who amongst you will lead you from this point forward. You all spent an entire day in hell together yesterday and should be familiar with each other well enough to have a good idea of who has the potential to be a good leader. Choose wisely."

The instructors divided the group into four squads and instructed each squad to select a squad leader, then the entire group elected an overall platoon commander from the four squad leaders. With the leaders chosen, the drill instructors pulled them aside and laid out their responsibilities as squad leaders and platoon commander. Squad leaders were charged with conducting roll call and reporting any issues to the platoon commander. The platoon commander then relayed everything to the drill sergeants.

"This is your chain of command," Benning said, addressing the platoon after all was settled with the leader selections. "If you have any questions, concerns, whatever, you must utilize your chain of command. You tell your squad leader. If he can't handle your problem, he will pass it to the platoon commander. If the platoon commander can't solve it, he will then come to us. From this point forward, the only person who should be coming to our office is the platoon commander."

At the end of the day, after Benning dismissed the platoon, the recruits all began changing out of their uniforms and putting their civilian clothes back on. The drill sergeants were a little confused and thought the men didn't understand the uniforms were there's to keep.

"Tell them to keep their uniforms on. They need to wear them home every night and tell the mother fuckers to wash them, too. I ain't their damn momma! They think they're gonna leave them here for me to do their fucking laundry? They wear them home, wash them, and then wear them back in the morning."

Fahdi quickly translated this to the new platoon commander who quickly and impressively whipped his men back into a sharp formation. The platoon commander conferred with his squad leaders for a minute and then addressed Benning.

"He is asking if it would be alright for them to wear civilian clothes off base. He said they will take the uniforms home in their bags and bring them back in the mornings to change into after they arrive. They don't want people in town to know they are training with the Americans. It's not safe for them," Fahdi explained.

Benning was taken a little aback by this. "Well, do they understand that upon graduation and becoming members of the ICDC they will be required to wear a uniform at *all times*? Soldiers can't dress in civilian clothing."

"Yes, they understand," Fahdi replied. "But he says when they signed up, Captain Rowe and his guys told them if they passed the training they would be assigned to different areas of the country, where hopefully no one will know who they are."

Benning granted the trainees permission to wear their civilian clothes to and from base, but told the platoon commander the men were still responsible for washing their uniforms every night. "For every recruit I smell nasty B.O. on, I will personally take it out of *your* ass!" he barked at the platoon commander.

After a few days, the recruits started warming up to Fahdi and the other translators, mainly because they usually ate lunch with the trainees out in the yard while the drill sergeants took their lunch in their office. Captain Rowe had contracted a local restaurant to provide lunch for the men each day, which was not only a bonus for the recruits but for the translators as well who were more than happy to get a free Iraqi meal to balance out all the American-style food they got on base. Although it was a delicious treat at first, the greasy chow hall food began doing a number on Fahdi's stomach. He'd quickly learned bacon was something to enjoy in delicate moderation.

While Fahdi was eating lunch on the third day of the training, a couple of the recruits sat down near him and struck up a conversation. They introduced themselves and one asked, "So what's the U.S. like?"

Fahdi furrowed his brow in confusion and simply replied, "How should I know?"

The two recruits exchanged bemused looks.

In the trainees' defense, Fahdi is rather light skinned, in comparison to the average Iraqi, and has electric green eyes, a rare trait amongst Mid-Easterners. Not only did they think Fahdi had come to Iraq from the U.S. with the military, but that he was simply an American who spoke fluent Arabic. Informing them about not being an American and never having been to the U.S., Fahdi's new friends asked where he was from—sure, at least, he wasn't from the immediate area.

Fahdi hesitated, not wanting to tell them he was from Baghdad, and simply said, "From up north near Kurdistan."

"Are you Kurdish?" one of them asked.

"No, I'm from one of the villages outside Mosul."

Fahdi got along well with most of the recruits and even became friends with a few. But as Benning's primary mouthpiece, he had to yell and scream in their faces constantly, which tended to strain his relationship with some of the guys.

"No matter what, I wasn't going to stick up for any of them. Sometimes, when Benning was screaming at one of them for no reason, a recruit would give me a look like, 'Seriously, dude?' but I wasn't about to question Benning or any of the other drill sergeants. Most of the guys understood, but some didn't take it too well. I didn't care, though. Keeping my job was worth a hell of a lot more to me than hurting anyone's feelings."

Fahdi was making friends on the American side of the base as well. In the evenings, he'd started visiting the gym and made a couple of regular workout buddies. He also hung out often in the base rec room where he competed in marathon rounds of *Call of Duty* on PlayStation with the U.S. soldiers.

Living with the Americans, he learned a lot about the culture and picked up the various nuances of the young American military enlisted men. Fahdi wasn't a smoker but he often joined the soldiers when they took their regular "smoke breaks" just to chit-chat and they'd offer him cigarettes. In the beginning, he politely declined, but one day decided to take one of the offerings. Sadly, to this day, Fahdi smokes two packs a day.

Some of the soldiers were just as interested in Fahdi as he was in learning about them and their life in the U.S.

During a smoke break one evening, one of the soldiers asked, "So what do you guys do for fun?"

"Yeah, do they have any nightclubs around here?" another piped in.

"Or how about strip clubs?" a third asked with a sly smile.

"Why? Are you guys planning to sneak out for a night-on-the-town in Fallujah?" Fahdi replied facetiously.

"What about weed? Do you have any of that here?" another soldier asked, a little more quietly than the others.

This question tripped Fahdi up. Not familiar with the term "weed," he looked confused about what the soldier was asking.

"You know, *weed*," the soldier pressed. "You smoke it to get high, man. Drugs, dude."

Fahdi knew what "drugs" were and a flash of recognition shot across his face. "Oh right . . . I mean, no. No drugs. If you got caught doing drugs under Saddam, you got executed. Publicly, as in your body hanging in the street for a few days as a warning to what happens," Fahdi added nonchalantly.

That put an end to the "cultural sharing" for the evening.

Although Fahdi was getting used to the average soldier's twisted sense of humor and the extremely foul language they all used with their friends, Fahdi was traumatized by the blatant nudity he was subjected to on a nightly basis during "shower time."

"They would walk across the base butt-ass naked between the tents and the shower trailers," Fahdi described. "At first, I thought they were doing it to mess with me."

The first few times Fahdi had showered at the base, it was late at night and the shower trailers had been relatively empty. Reporting for duty at 6 a.m., he found himself needing to go to bed earlier and, therefore, needing to shower earlier.

While standing at the sink brushing his teeth one evening, a large soldier walked in the shower trailer, dropped his bathroom bag on the sink right next to Fahdi and then proceeded to strip completely naked while standing a mere few inches from Fahdi.

"I just froze," Fahdi smiled, embarrassed. "I didn't want to look at him—stared straight ahead—and continued to brush my teeth, but I was totally eyeballing him out the corner of my eye. I thought maybe he took his clothes off outside the shower because he was such a big guy and couldn't maneuver enough inside the tight shower stall. Nope. He stripped butt-ass naked and then pulled out his shaving kit and started shaving."

Still frozen with his toothbrush hanging out of his mouth, another soldier entered the shower trailer and walked up to the sink on the other side of Fahdi. He, too, proceeded to remove all his clothing and then started brushing his teeth.

"I thought, *Holy shit, is this some kind of conspiracy or sick American joke?*" Fahdi said. "I was sure the bastards were fucking with me."

Nearly in a panic, Fahdi quickly shoved his toiletries back in his bag and hightailed it out of the shower trailer. Halfway back to the barracks he realized he hadn't taken a shower, but decided it was better to get up at 2 a.m. to shower every night to avoid such situations.

About a week into the training, Benning pulled Fahdi aside one afternoon. "What did I tell you the first day we met?" Benning snapped in a threatening tone.

"Uh, a lot of stuff," Fahdi replied befuddled.

"Smartass. I explicitly told you to translate everything I say; exactly what I say and how I say it."

"I am," Fahdi defended.

Unbeknownst to Fahdi, Benning had one of the other terps eavesdropping on Fahdi throughout the morning to relay his performance as a translator.

"No, you're not. You're not cussing at the recruits. You're sugarcoating everything."

"Look, they already know you're cussing at them," Fahdi defended himself. "They understand what 'fuck,' 'shit,' and 'asshole,' are. Trust me, you're getting you're point across. Me reiterating it again in Arabic is only going to rub them the wrong way and cause problems. Cussing at these people isn't going to get you anywhere. They don't respond to cussing the way Americans do. These people already don't like you too much as it is. Talking down to them and insulting them isn't going to help your mission."

"The only reason I'm going to let this slide is because you're a good terp," Benning said dropping the subject. "But you're a cocky little shit and a smartass."

The final few days of boot camp consisted of weapons training, culminating in a trip to the weapons range on the American side of the base where the recruits would do their weapons qualifications.

As the weapons training phase began, Fahdi could tell Benning and his men were a little on edge and extremely cautious. There had been several incidents in Afghanistan where local recruits being trained by U.S. forces had turned on their American instructors and gunned them down. Benning wasn't taking any chances. Each recruit was issued an AK-47 and a .9mm (no ammo) to use during the training that had to be turned back in and catalogued at the end of each day. The drill sergeants also started frisking the recruits every morning before they entered the base to ensure no one tried to smuggle in any ammunition.

The trainees were taught how to disassemble both weapons and properly clean them, safe handling methods, and tactical strategies. Most of the recruits had been handling AKs since they were old enough to walk, making weapons training much easier. Even though this was evident, Benning refused to deviate from protocol and went through all the basics, strictly following the training outline developed by the Army to the letter.

"I'd never seen any of the U.S. military guys with an AK-47. They predominately used M-16s or M-4s, but Benning and his guys were completely proficient with the AK. They definitely knew their shit."

The final day of boot camp was the one and only day the recruits were given live ammunition. Fahdi hardly recognized the drill sergeants that morning. They were in full battle dress: body armor, helmets, pistols strapped to their legs, and M-16s slung across their backs. Each of them had also donned a stony glare conveying a simple message: I dare you to test me, mother fucker. Again, Benning wasn't taking any chances.

"I was sure someone was going to make a stupid mistake and get shot," Fahdi recalled. "If someone had so much as sneezed too loudly out on that range, I'm sure Benning and his guys would have killed us all."

Not only were the drill instructors going to the range armed, they were even issuing the translators .9mms to carry for the day. The other two translators were U.S. residents who'd lived in the states for many years, but Fahdi was a little shocked when Benning handed him a pistol, too. He was as much a local Iraqi as the recruits.

"I trust you more than I trust any of these other mother fuckers I'm about to hand AKs and pistols to today," Benning said in response to Fahdi's surprised look. The minute everyone was out on the range, he explained to all the translators he wanted them to continuously circulate throughout the group watching and listening for any suspicious activity or chatter. "You hear, see, or even smell anything funny, you tell me or one of my guys immediately," Benning ordered. "And if we start shooting, you start shooting."

The recruits lined up in formation at the range and Benning addressed the platoon before issuing the weapons. "You will be handed a weapon," Benning announced. "That weapon is to be aimed either at the ground or at your target downrange at all times."

Since pistols were easy to conceal and difficult for the instructors to maintain visuals on, the recruits were only given AK-47s to use at the range.

"If any of you as much as grips your weapon in a suspicious manner, making me or any of my men uncomfortable in any way, we will put you on the ground," Benning warned. "You are not to speak at all while holding a weapon; not to me, not to any of the instructors, not to any of the translators, and not to any other recruit. If you need to ask a question or even need to clear your fucking throat, you are to place your weapon on the ground facing downrange and then request permission to speak by raising your right hand."

When Benning finished giving the instructions, the drill sergeants divided the platoon into groups of six. There would only be six active shooters at a time, one for each of Benning's six drill sergeants to keep an eye on, freeing Benning up to patrol the entire group and give the firing commands. The recruits were only handed the live ammo when it was their turn at the target. The recruits would take their position, then the drill sergeants approached them from behind and handed three magazines to the recruits over their left shoulder. The recruits were to remain facing downrange, at all times, while a drill sergeant covered them from behind. Each of the three magazines contained thirty rounds. The first magazine was for semi-automatic fire—one trigger pull, one shot. The recruits were ordered to fire ten rounds from a standing position, then ten rounds from a kneeling position, and the final ten rounds from the prone (lying on the ground) position. For the second magazine, the recruits were directed to fire in three-round-bursts—again, ten

AMANDA MATTI

standing, ten kneeling, and ten prone. The third magazine was for fully-automatic fire. Although harder to control, the recruits were again instructed to do their best to fire ten standing, ten kneeling, and ten prone.

The first group of shooters consisted of the platoon commander, squad leaders, and two other respected recruits who had been former officers in the Iraqi Army. Benning sent these guys up first as they were already familiar with basic military range protocol and he hoped they'd set a good example for the other recruits on how to conduct themselves. Benning barked through the commands and the group fired their ninety rounds.

Placing their weapons on the ground, Benning and the other instructors were visibly impressed by the shooting skills the first group demonstrated. But considering they were seasoned military officers, Benning expected these men to know their way around a rifle.

The recruits in the second group of shooters were all "newbies," young guys with no military background. Completing their firing drills, the American instructors were even more amazed. All six hit the target with all ninety rounds.

"Jesus Christ," Benning muttered, half to himself and half to Fahdi, "nobody misses."

"These guys have been shooting since they were five," Fahdi commented. "It's not like there's much to do for fun around here. Instead of mastering PlayStation, they master AK-47s."

Every single recruit passed weapons qualifications.

Back on the training base, the recruits were issued their official military uniforms and gear, and were ordered to practice their marching and formations for the following day's graduation ceremony.

* * *

Captain Rowe attended the graduation ceremony, along with several other U.S. Army officers who would serve as advisors to the new ICDC platoon and continue training them in the ways of U.S. military tactics and procedures. The new graduates would have to wait for the next group to go through their training before there would be enough new ICDC soldiers to form the full company Rowe needed. Once complete, he planned to ship the company off to fight as a functioning unit alongside U.S. military forces in another area of the country, just as he'd promised.

Rowe came for graduation with his own translator and addressed the new soldiers. "Gentlemen, you are the first ICDC members of Al-Anbar Province. You are the first platoon of what will soon be the 1st Company of the 1st Brigade of the Al-Anbar Division of the Iraqi Civil Defense Corp. Remember that men. You *are* the first of the first. This is a great achievement and an accomplishment of which you should be extremely proud. From this day forward, your mission is to establish and maintain the security of your country, your home. Wear these uniforms with pride as you protect the people of Iraq and help to rebuild this great nation."

"It was an inspiring speech, but I don't think Captain Rowe fully believed the words coming from his own mouth. He knew full well as soon as the new soldiers stepped outside the gate, they'd strip off those shiny new uniforms, stuff them into their bags, and return home in flip flops and jeans. They all simply wanted him to shut up and get the graduation over with because at the close of the ceremony, they'd receive their first paycheck. The overwhelming sentiment amongst the group was less, 'I'm so proud of my accomplishments,' and more along the lines of, 'Shut up and give us our fucking money.' But Captain Rowe was a long-term thinker and knew things weren't going to change overnight with the first group of 100 ICDC soldiers. His plan was to turn things around with sheer force in numbers. One hundred soldiers would soon be 1,000, and he had faith that 1,000 ICDC soldiers would be a lot more likely to keep their uniforms on."

Unfortunately, Captain Rowe was up against an enemy who was building numbers faster than Benning and his instructors could churn out new ICDC soldiers. The foothold Al-Qaeda and the insurgency had in Al-Anbar province was gaining strength with each passing day. Nearby Ramadi was already full of foreign fighters pouring in from Syria, Jordan, Lebanon, Saudi Arabia, and Libya; all coming to defend Islam from the invading infidels.

"It got to the point in Ramadi, if you were walking down the street and happened to cross paths with an American convoy or patrol, if you were even caught looking at them, the insurgency would probably come after you. You fucking turned around and walked in the other direction. Better yet, you crossed over and took a different street entirely. Getting caught associating with the Americans could very well be a death sentence."

At that time, foreign fighters began trickling into Western Iraq, luring the poorer Iraqis of the rural areas to open their cities and homes by offering great sums of money. A group of four fighters would offer a family a colossal $1,000 in U.S. currency to rent a room in their house for a month. This was more than what a lot of people earned in a year.

"When you need food and basic necessities for your children, you'll accept money from the devil himself. At first, they were decent houseguests—quiet, minded their own business—but they were like a bad virus. As time went on and their numbers grew, they turned on the population. They were no longer paying for the room they rented in your neighbor's house, they were now threatening to kill his kids if he didn't let them stay there. The security situation in the area was crumbling and Ramadi and nearby Fallujah were ticking time bombs."

CHAPTER SEVEN

BAMBOOZLERS, BACKSTABBERS & BOREDOM

MARCH 2004

After the first group of ICDC soldiers graduated, Captain Rowe gave the drill sergeants and their translators a four-day break before having them start training the second cycle. Fahdi relished his first two days off. He slept in, played marathon rounds of video games at the rec room, and enjoyed prolonged workout sessions at the gym. But by the third day, boredom set in. He decided to mosey over to Captain Rowe's office to see if he had any odd jobs Fahdi could do for him. Rowe happily put him right to work. Rowe's personal translator happened to have the next two days off so he was in need of a fill-in terp.

Now that Rowe had finished recruiting enough men to hopefully end up with a company of 194 ICDC soldiers, as soon as the second group of recruits finished their training, he was busily working on his next mission, acquiring vehicles for the new soldiers. The Army didn't want the new ICDC soldiers driving around in U.S. Humvees, so they gave Captain Rowe a budget to purchase vehicles from the local area. Some of the newly graduated ICDC officers were assisting Rowe in this venture and Rowe asked Fahdi to help translate at a meeting with a couple of the officers later that afternoon.

"The ICDC officers had developed quite a lucrative little racket. They were buying trucks from locals in the area who had stolen the vehicles from former Iraqi military bases in the area. The officers would buy the trucks for around $1,000 each from the locals and then sell them to Rowe for $5,000. They were making a killing. Rowe would hand them hard cash and take the trucks. When I caught on to what the officers were doing, I thought Captain Rowe was, at best, naïve or just plain stupid.

"However, I had greatly underestimated him. I later learned Captain Rowe was an extremely intelligent quick study. He learned how to read Iraqis faster than any American I've ever met."

After watching Captain Rowe shell out nearly $100,000 to purchase various trucks and military type vehicles from the officers over the next week or so, Fahdi could no longer stand idly by and decided to speak up.

After finishing a day of training with the drill sergeants, Fahdi stopped by Captain Rowe's office on the way back to his tent. Mustering courage, her stated, "You do realize these vehicles are government vehicles that were stolen and are being sold back to you, right? They technically already belong to you, or at least to the ICDC."

Captain Rowe smiled knowingly and simply replied, "No shit, Sherlock. I'm well-aware of the situation, but thanks for the heads up."

"Then why are you paying these assholes for the trucks?" Fahdi asked confused. "Just fucking take them!"

"If we don't buy these vehicles, someone else will," Rowe divulged cryptically. "You catch my drift?"

Fahdi remained silent.

"Buying them back from the locals makes the people happy, keeps the insurgency or terrorists from getting a hold of them, and makes us happy. Rolling in and confiscating them by force would not make people happy. We would essentially be stealing from the people since the vehicles have already been stolen and are now in the hands of the people. The last thing we want to do is piss the locals off and subsequently drive them into the arms of the resistance. Do you get it now?"

Fahdi felt a little sheepish. "Yep, it makes perfect sense, sir. I apologize for questioning you. It was not my place to do so."

"No, I'm glad you spoke up. It's a hell of a lot more than many of your fellow countrymen would do for us. You're all right. Now go away," Rowe replied, reverting to his typical callous tone and flicking his hand in a shooing manner. "I've got a lot of shit to do."

Rowe's second group of recruits graduated, and although there were enough to form the company, he wasn't stopping there. He already had another complete third group ready to start training and planned to have a fourth ready in time to start immediately after them. Rowe again granted Benning and his team four days of R&R (rest and relaxation) before starting the third cycle. Fahdi planned to utilize all four days this time and go home to Baghdad, but the logistics of getting home proved more difficult than Fahdi expected.

Captain Rowe said the only way he could get a ride to Baghdad was to find an open seat on one of the convoys heading there. Sadly, none were scheduled to leave for Baghdad until the following week. Fahdi couldn't wait that long. He'd have to figure out his own travel arrangements.

The road between Ramadi and Baghdad was becoming more treacherous by the day, especially for a translator working for the U.S. military. Fahdi had heard about several local translators from their base who'd been murdered while in Ramadi. An Army unit discovered the body of one of the executed translators while out on a routine patrol one day and the news spread like wildfire.

Fahdi decided to call a friend of his who was originally from Ramadi to see if he knew of anyone in the area that could give him a ride to Baghdad. As luck would have it, his friend happened to be in Ramadi for the weekend visiting his family. He planned to head back to Baghdad that evening anyway and was happy to give Fahdi a ride. Fahdi walked into town and met up with his friend at a local café.

"Of course, he asked what I was doing in Ramadi. I didn't trust anyone and made up some elaborate story about how I'd come with another friend to visit his mom and we'd only planned to stay a couple of days, but his mom had gotten sick. He'd decided to stay longer, but I had to get back to Baghdad. I guess I was convincing enough. He didn't question me about it beyond that."

Fahdi spent most of his four-day weekend sleeping. When it was time to head back to Ramadi, his mother was a nervous wreck and begged him not to return. He assured her his job was completely innocuous and he remained safe within the heavily protected walls of the American base.

"Please promise me you'll quit as soon as it gets dangerous," his mother pleaded.

"I promise."

Fahdi's brother gave him a ride back to Ramadi and dropped him off in a random area of town. Fahdi walked back to the base, praying with every step he'd make it before attracting unwanted attention from any of the locals, knowing it would be the last time he'd be able to walk around alone outside the base. Any cover he had was now blown.

Not wanting to risk entering the base after dark, Fahdi cut his time at home a little short to ensure he made it back to Ramadi by early afternoon. Stopping by the PX before heading to his barracks, he happened to bump into Sergeant Benning who was shopping for supplies for a barbeque he the other drill sergeants were having in celebration of their last day off before resuming boot camp training. The third group of recruits started the next day. Benning invited Fahdi to join them and he accepted, but felt a little out of place when he arrived and realized he was the *only* translator they'd invited to their little shindig.

"You're a good dude, Fahdi," Benning commented somewhat out of the blue at the barbeque. The remark caught Fahdi totally off guard. Benning wasn't big on handing out compliments.

"Oh, well . . . thank you," Fahdi replied cautiously, wondering if he was being set up for a prank.

"No, seriously," Benning reiterated.

"Ok," Fahdi said, unsure how to take Benning's compliment.

"I'm serious mother fucker!" Benning barked. "You're cool and a good terp . . . once you started showing up to work on time," he added sardonically before taking a big swig from a Red Bull.

Benning retreated into his tent and came back holding a large, sheathed KA-BAR military knife. "Here, I've been meaning to give this to you," he said casually, handing Fahdi the knife.

"Oh, wow," Fahdi said with a huge grin. "Thank you. This is awesome."

"Good, glad you like it," Benning replied coolly. "Now tuck it in your waistband before someone sees it."

Fahdi quickly did as Benning instructed, remembering locals weren't authorized to have blades longer than three inches on base.

The following evening, Fahdi was enjoying a cigarette outside his barracks when one of the local Iraqis, who was part of the base janitorial crew, joined him. An older man from Ramadi, he'd been hired to do odd jobs around the base such as change trash cans, sweep common areas, and other miscellaneous work. There were a couple hundred locals employed on the base janitorial crew as part of the Army's efforts to "make friends." Fahdi had seen the old man around on nearly a daily basis since he started working there and the two had chitchatted often while taking smoke breaks together over the past few weeks.

"He was just a nice old man who I kind of felt bad for. I'd often seen him hauling heavy trash or doing other manual labor out in the heat. Sometimes I would give him a water bottle or he'd take a break and we'd share a cigarette."

As the old man approached, Fahdi noticed he had a somber look on his face, which was out of the ordinary for this typically jovial man who always seemed to be smiling. Fahdi offered him a cigarette but the man politely declined.

"I need to tell you something," the old man said solemnly. "There are photocopies of your American Titan badge with all of your information and picture posted in several of the mosques across Ramadi. They have yours and copies of about a dozen other translators who work here at the base. They have you all labeled as 'traitors' and are offering a reward to anyone who brings you to the mosque—dead or alive."

At first Fahdi thought the old man was playing a sick joke. But after staring him down for several long seconds, he knew he was telling the truth. Fahdi's realization was reinforced when the old man recited Fahdi's full name and badge number.

"I was afraid you wouldn't believe me, so I memorized your name and badge number to prove it to you," the old man said. "These people aren't playing around and they're getting more powerful every day. The Americans won't be able to protect you forever. They are threatening anyone who associates with the U.S. military—the new ICDC soldiers, translators, cleaners, construction workers . . . Hell, even a guy who used to sell water to the soldiers while on patrol in his neighborhood was found murdered a few days ago. I am quitting my job here tomorrow, and I suggest you do the same. The only reason I'm coming back tomorrow is to collect my pay for the last two weeks. I tried to get them to give it to me today, but they refused. I need that money to feed my family for the next couple of weeks while I look for a new job."

Fahdi had heard that a week prior, a dozen of the newly graduated ICDC soldiers from the second group had been murdered execution style in Ramadi. In response, Captain Rowe had the Army erect tents, build some makeshift barracks, and park a couple of shower trailers on the ICDC side of the camp to keep the soldiers safely on base until it was time for them to ship off to join units in other parts of the country.

No surprise, Captain Rowe's recruiting efforts had also become a lot more difficult lately. The $150 a month salary was no longer a large enough incentive in the face of the insurgency's legitimate threats to slaughter the families of anyone who signed up for the ICDC training. The U.S. had won the war, but was quickly losing the peace.

Fahdi seriously considered the old man's suggestion and contemplated quitting right then and there. The fact the copy was in color was even more detrimental to Fahdi. His green eyes and light skin made him easier to identify out on the street. Ultimately though, his anger outweighed his fear, as did his desire to expose and seek revenge against the asshole who had betrayed him and the other translators. No, he refused to run.

He thanked the old man for the heads up, but asked him for one more favor. "Is there any way you could snatch one of the photocopies and bring it with you tomorrow? Preferably one of mine, but if not, one with any of the translators here at the base will work. I need to show it to the Captain I work for and the Titan representative so they can see for themselves what's going on."

The old man said he'd try but couldn't promising anything.

The old man came through for Fahdi, though, and handed over a copy of one of Fahdi's own "wanted" posters the following afternoon. After that, Fahdi never saw him again. Just as the old man had described, the poster was of moderate quality, an 8x10 color photocopy of the front of Fahdi's Titan translator badge. He took the copy straight to Captain Rowe, who was less than sympathetic to Fahdi's plight.

"What's the Army going to do about this?" Fahdi asked impatiently as Rowe examined it.

"All we can do is continue to offer you refuge here on the base; that is, of course, as long as you continue to be employed by the U.S. military or one of its subsidiaries," Rowe answered matter-of-factly.

"So now I'm an indentured servant," Fahdi declared, somewhat shocked. "As long as I continue working for you, you'll protect me from these assholes who are trying to kill me for helping you. But if I quit, I'm on my own. Am I right?"

"Look, we've launched an investigation to try and find out where the leak came from."

"Wait! You knew about this and didn't warn me?"

"One of the other translators alerted the base security office several days ago that he'd heard from someone who'd heard from someone that these posters were out in the town," Rowe explained. "We didn't tell anyone because the information was on a need-to-know basis, and the less people who knew about it, the easier it would be to find the leak."

"I was walking alone through the streets of Ramadi two days ago, completely unaware there was a price on my head!" Fahdi shouted. "That's pretty fucking need-to-know!" Fahdi stormed out of Rowe's office, slamming the door behind him.

In the end, the investigation into the leak of the translators' identities and Titan badges led to a Palestinian-American linguist who was also employed with Titan. As a U.S. citizen, he'd been granted a low-level security clearance and worked in the Titan office on the base. When the Titan translators would visit the office to collect their monthly pay or simply ask a question, he'd have them hand over their Titan badges for him to "verify" their employment and he'd make a quick photocopy of the badge. Since he wasn't an Iraqi and had come over from the U.S., he wasn't authorized to leave the base, so it was likely he'd been colluding with one of the locals who worked on the base, either a local translator like Fahdi or someone from the janitorial or construction crew.

Locals were searched both coming and going from the base, so Fahdi suspected the photocopies had likely been smuggled out in someone's underwear. Rumor had it the mole had also been well compensated for his troubles. Word around base was a search of his bunk area in the barracks uncovered nearly $10,000 in cash hidden in the inner lining of a rucksack he'd purchased at the base PX.

Of the terps whose identities had been sold to the insurgency, about half decided to quit and returned to their hometowns.

The rest took the Army's advice and remained within the walls of the base at all times unless they were traveling to Baghdad, and then they were sure to hitch a ride with a convoy. Sadly, a couple of the translators were 'stuck between a rock and a hard place.'

They were from Ramadi or areas nearby and had no choice but to either never return home or take their chances. Within a month of the leak, two of the translators whose identities had been compromised were dead. Fahdi knew them both. Sadly, they were only the first in a long line of fellow translators he'd encountered throughout his time working as a linguist for the Americans that were murdered for "aiding the infidels."

One afternoon, toward the end of the cycle for the third group of recruits, Captain Rowe sent one of the soldiers on his staff over to the training camp to pick up Fahdi and take him to the Titan office on base. There, the Titan representative told him to go pack up his stuff. He was being transferred the following day.

At first Fahdi was excited, hoping he was being transferred back to Baghdad. But his joy was short-lived. The rep told him he was going to Camp Manhattan in Habbaniyah, a small town down the road halfway between Ramadi and Fallujah, and had to catch a ride with a convoy heading out at 7 a.m. the next day. They would drop him off at Manhattan on their way to Baghdad.

Fahdi knew it was futile to argue and headed to his barracks to pack up his belongings.

"They had us local translators by the balls at that point. We couldn't risk getting fired by refusing an assignment or we'd be kicked off the base, then probably end up dead. And we couldn't threaten to quit, we'd be kicked off the base and, again, end up dead. We were stuck and they knew it, and they exploited our situation."

At 6:30 the next morning, Fahdi was standing outside his tent enjoying a final cigarette before heading to meet up with the convoy—no smoking allowed while riding with them—when he was practically tackled from behind.

"What the *fuck* are you doing?" Sergeant Benning's angry voice screamed in Fahdi's ear. "Do you know what time it is mother fucker? Did you fall on your head last night or something, asshole? What did I tell you about being on time? You were just starting to get your shit together."

It was then and there Fahdi learned that communication within the U.S. military was extremely poor and essentially nonexistent between the military and its subsidiaries. He assumed Captain Rowe had been apprised of his impending transfer and had passed the info on to Benning—wrong.

"Hey, whoa!" Fahdi shrieked, regaining his footing. "Captain Rowe didn't tell you?"

"Tell me what *asshole*?" Benning snapped.

"I don't work with you anymore. They're transferring me to Habbaniyah today."

Benning's eyes bulged in shock and bewilderment. "Is that some sort of fucking joke?"

"I swear to God," Fahdi blurted raising his right hand. "Ask Captain Rowe."

"They can't transfer you in the middle of a fucking training cycle!"

"Hey, I just work here."

"Don't move, I'll be right back," Benning ordered and double-timed it to Captain Rowe's office.

"Hey, I have to go meet the convoy!" Fahdi called after Benning. "They're leaving in twenty minutes!"

"*Don't! Fucking! Move!*" Benning hollered back without breaking stride.

Fahdi threw his hands up and shook his head in frustration.

Fifteen minutes later, about to grab his bag and go catch his ride with the convoy, Benning reappeared.

"Captain Rowe is meeting with the Titan assholes right now," Benning relayed. "He's going to try and talk them into delaying your transfer at least until we've finished the current group's cycle. Rowe told me to tell you to sit tight here and wait for further instructions. I gotta' get over to the camp and I expect to see you there shortly."

Fahdi never saw Sergeant Benning again.

Ten minutes later, one of the civilian managers from the Titan office pulled up in front of Fahdi's tent in a white pickup truck and rolled down his window. "Get your shit and get in," he ordered in an irritated tone. Fahdi obliged without hesitation.

"May I ask where you're taking me?" Fahdi ventured cautiously.

"I'm taking you to catch your fucking ride to Camp Manhattan," the Titan manager replied sternly. "They're holding up the entire convoy waiting for you."

"I'm sorry, but my boss, Sergeant Benning, told me—"

"*I'm your boss!*" the Titan manager roared. "You work for *us* not *them*. You do what *we* tell you to do, *when* we tell you to do it! Those arrogant fucks think they own and are in command of everyone," he added, more to himself than to Fahdi.

There was a power struggle going on between the U.S. Army and Titan on a much larger level than Fahdi's petty transfer, and he was smart enough not to get in the middle of it. Fahdi kept his mouth shut and simply went where he was told, when he was told.

When the convoy deposited Fahdi at Camp Manhattan's front gate, he had no clue what unit he was supposed to report to or even who to ask for. He told the soldiers on watch duty at the gate who he was, showed them his Titan badge, and told them he'd been ordered to report to Camp Manhattan for duty but that was all he knew. Of course, the soldiers had no idea where Fahdi was supposed to go, but they at least offered him shelter in one of the small guard shack trailers by the gate, telling him he could hang out there until someone figured out who he was supposed to report to. Fahdi ended up "hanging out" in that trailer for two days before someone finally came for him.

"I fucking hated that base," Fahdi recalled with his face scrunched in disgust. "It was a total shithole compared to the luxury of Camp Ramadi and its five-star chow hall."

It was at this point Fahdi had his first experience with MREs (meal ready to eat). Since he wasn't allowed to enter the base for those first couple of days, the gate guards would drop MREs off at the trailer for him several times a day. At first, he was *not* happy about the MREs and was anxious to be granted access to the base so he could eat real food again, but he soon discovered Manhattan's chow hall didn't even cook its own food. All their food was shipped in from the large TQ Airbase a few miles down the road.

"I'm pretty sure they just scraped together all the leftovers from the TQ chow hall and drove them over to Manhattan. By the time we got the food, it was cold and nasty. After a couple of meals at their crappy chow hall, I was happy to continue living off MREs for the duration of my stay at Manhattan, and actually discovered several varieties I thoroughly enjoyed."

Finally, an Army officer, Lieutenant Grey, showed up and told Fahdi he'd been assigned to work with one of the EOD units operating out of Camp Manhattan.

"I didn't know what EOD stood for, but I had a bad feeling. It turned out to be even worse than I'd feared. It wasn't until two days later I found out EOD stood for Explosive Ordinance Disposal. In other words, the poor bastards whose job it was to hunt down IEDs."

IEDs (Improvised Explosive Devices) are typically homemade

bombs that are usually buried in shallow holes on the side of the road and then detonated via a remote, often a cellphone, as military vehicles pass by. As of 2012, IEDs were the top killer of U.S. troops in Iraq.

Fahdi was shown to a small Conex trailer that would serve as his barracks, which, much to his delight, was a step up from the communal tent he'd slept in at Ramadi.

At 5 a.m. the next morning, there was a knock on his trailer door. He answered and one of the soldiers in the EOD unit Fahdi now worked for handed Fahdi a U.S. Army desert camouflage uniform, combat boots, a helmet, and body armor.

"You can keep the uniform and boots, but the body armor and helmet need to be turned in to the unit at the end of each day," the soldier informed Fahdi in an emotionless tone. "Get dressed and meet us at the front gate. We're on patrol today."

"I was really proud to get to wear an official Army uniform and was excited to put it on." Fahdi smiled with fond remembrance. "It almost made up for the hell I was about to go through. Almost."

Fahdi changed into his uniform, doing his best to properly tuck in and blouse the pant legs around his boots the way he'd seen U.S. soldiers wear theirs over the last year. Once he felt he'd successfully mimicked the proper American soldier-style, he left to go meet up with the EOD convoy, walking a little taller as he crossed the base.

As usual, everyone was ready and waiting for Fahdi. One of the soldiers told him to get inside one of the unit's M2 Bradley tanks. The crew sealed the tank and Fahdi didn't see the light of day for the next eight hours.

"They didn't tell me anything; no one said a single word to me all day. I spent the entire day jostling around inside a stifling, metal box. It was hot and miserable," Fahdi said, shaking his head. "I didn't know where we were or what we were doing. At one point, I tried to ask one of the crew members where we were going, but got no answer. I just gave up and did my best to 'roll with it.' I felt like a kidnap victim being hauled around in the trunk of a car. We'd move and then stop for some time, move again, and stop, over and over. It was the most boring fucking job I've ever had in my life, especially since they really had no need for a translator. They just needed a terp with them in case they happened to come across any locals."

Due to the oppressive heat inside the Bradley, Fahdi perspired profusely and, consequently, devoured several large bottles of water over the course of the morning. As the tank came to one of its stops, Fahdi asked if he could hop out and relieve his bladder. He was promptly informed no one was authorized to exit the vehicle while out on patrol. One of the soldiers tossed an empty water bottle in Fahdi's lap and told him to pee in it.

"I'd never peed in a bottle before and I sure as hell wasn't going to try it for the first time in that metal box, in front of those guys who obviously didn't like me too much as it was, so I just held it."

Around one o'clock in the afternoon, the unit made a lunch stop at TQ Airbase and Fahdi was granted permission to exit the tank to stretch his legs and use the restroom. He made a beeline for a nearby row of porta potties, sure he was within mere minutes of his bladder exploding.

The unit dined on MREs for lunch and was back out on patrol within the hour. The two full MREs Fahdi scoffed down for lunch, combined with even hotter afternoon temperatures, converged to instigate a new malady for Fahdi as he was pitched around inside the Bradley—severe motion sickness. Fahdi may not have learned how to pee in an empty water bottle that day, but he did master the art of vomiting in one.

Soon after sunset, the unit again stopped in TQ for a quick dinner of more MREs. Fahdi elected to forgo his meal that evening but was thankful to be able to get out of the tank and stretch his legs again.

Following the dinner break, they were back out on patrol well into the night. The unit finally called it a day and returned to Camp Manhattan around midnight. Fahdi literally crawled out of the belly of the Bradley and hobbled toward his trailer. *That's it, it's official. I'm quitting.* It was his first day of actual "Army life" and he was not interested in sticking around for a second.

Fahdi's unit had the next day off. There were two EOD teams at the camp that rotated, each working an eighteen-hour patrol, having every other day off. Fahdi had a mission to accomplish on his day off, though: find Lieutenant Grey and beg for a new post or, if the Lieutenant refused to transfer him, give his resignation.

Fahdi awoke ravenous. Having vomited everything he'd eaten the day before, he was more than ready to get something back in his stomach. He dined on a beef ravioli MRE and then set out to track down the Lieutenant.

Miraculously, he happened upon Lieutenant Grey on his way to the HQ tents. Not wanting to sound like a whiny bitch, Fahdi broached the subject from an operational perspective. "I'm really not doing anything with the EOD guys," Fahdi stated tactfully. "I just rode around in the Bradley all day yesterday. I feel completely useless. I really think I could contribute a lot more in a different position."

"Well, the unit has to have a terp with them at all times," the Lieutenant said. "It's simply protocol. Trust me, you are serving a purpose, an important one."

"I don't even know what's going on," Fahdi grumbled. "I spent eighteen hours in a tin can yesterday and the guys barely said two words to me the entire time." Lieutenant Grey smiled understandingly, then gave Fahdi a crash course on what EOD units did in general and his unit's particular mission in the area around Camp Manhattan. Feeling more informed but even more skeptical regarding his role, Fahdi concluded this job definitely fell into the "dangerous" category he'd promised to avoid.

To battle the boredom, Lieutenant Grey told Fahdi he could bring along a book, video game, magazine, etc. to occupy his time, or he could simply sleep all day if he wished. As far as the soldiers not talking to Fahdi, the Lieutenant tried to explain they were simply a little standoffish because they'd just met him and, yes, were a bit suspicious of all locals. Tension in the region had grown exponentially over the past couple of weeks. IEDs had become nearly a daily occurrence; sometimes multiple convoys were struck in a single day. The U.S. bases in the area were undergoing frequent mortar attacks and Fallujah had nearly reached a boiling point.

"I understand where you're coming from, Fahdi," the Lieutenant said. "But I really need you to stick with the EOD guys for at least a couple more days. A new batch of terps is supposed to arrive within the week. If you still want to transfer when they get here, I'll see what I can do."

"Thank you, sir," Fahdi replied with visible relief. "Have you ever worked with Marines?" Lieutenant Grey asked offhandedly.

Fahdi shook his head.

"I may have an alternate assignment for you. Give me a few days to research the details. I *can't* promise you it'll be any less dangerous, but I *can* promise you'll stay busy."

"I'm in," Fahdi declared. "Dangerous I can handle, mind-numbingly boring is unbearable."

Reluctantly, Fahdi was back at 5 a.m. the following morning to meet the EOD unit at the camp's front gate. The second morning with the EOD team was a carbon copy of the first—start, stop, no getting out, and no conversation. One of the most grueling aspects for Fahdi was not getting to take his usual cigarette breaks. No smoking in the tank.

They again stopped at the TQ Airbase for an MRE lunch and then were back on the road.

That afternoon, Fahdi experienced his first encounter with an IED and, no pun intended, it rocked his world.

"We were trolling along when suddenly there was the biggest, loudest, most ridiculous BOOM! I'd ever heard in my life." He peered directly into my eyes; blatant fear shining through to this day. "We were lucky in that it exploded before our tank got to it. The Bradley wasn't damaged, but the sound was unbelievable as it reverberated through the tank. I was sure it had ruptured my eardrums. After the explosion, it was mass chaos. There was gunfire and everyone was yelling. I don't think anyone was shooting at us, the soldiers were just firing randomly into the distance at anything that moved until the captain of the unit could calm everyone down and regain control of the situation. I had a splitting headache and was scared shitless for the rest of the day, but I was extremely thankful to be alive and uninjured."

Later on, one of the soldiers tossed a package of earplugs into Fahdi's lap. He then noticed everyone in the unit was wearing earplugs and it dawned on him why no one ever answered him when he'd tried talking to them.

"Thanks, but I really could have used these a little earlier," Fahdi said grudgingly.

"Oh, sorry dude," the soldier responded with a cynical smile.

Fahdi had officially survived initiation. An hour after the IED attack, it was like the clubhouse door opened up. By the end of the day, the guys were shooting-the-shit and cracking jokes with Fahdi like he'd always been one of the soldiers in the unit. Unfortunately, Fahdi would not get to stick around to enjoy his hard-earned acceptance.

CHAPTER EIGHT

MAJOR WARREN & THE MARINE CIVIL AFFAIRS UNIT

MARCH 2004

The very next evening, Lieutenant Grey showed up at Fahdi's trailer. "Great news," he announced as Fahdi opened the door. "You don't have to work with the EOD unit anymore. I've found you a new gig."

Although a little bittersweet, considering Fahdi had just broken through to the EOD's inner circle, he still wasn't excited about the actual work and was relieved to be assigned to a new position.

"Throw your boots on and come with me, I'll take you to meet your new team," the Lieutenant instructed.

On the walk across camp, Lieutenant Grey gave Fahdi a little info on his new assignment. The Unit was a six-man Marine Civil Affairs team headed up by a Major Travis Warren, Fahdi's new boss. The unit had arrived from the States earlier that day and planned to hit the ground running the following morning.

"I became a little anxious after learning I'd be working for a Major," Fahdi said. "It was the highest-ranking U.S. military officer I'd ever worked directly for. I remember thinking, *Oh shit, I better not fuck up.* Also, the fact that I'd be going out on patrols with him—a considerably high ranking military official—made me even more nervous because I'd be attached at the hip to a guy who'd have a huge bull's eye on his back."

Upon arrival at the Civil Affairs team's HQ tent, Lieutenant Grey introduced Fahdi to Major Warren, an all-American looking guy, a good six feet tall with sandy brown hair and intense blue-gray eyes.

Fahdi estimated his age to be mid-to late-thirties, but he had a kind, youthful smile that made him look ten years younger.

The Major offered some more details regarding his team's assignment.

"Our mission over the next few months here is to travel around the area, build and nurture relationships with the locals, and initiate reconstruction efforts in order to get life back to normal for the residents in and around Fallujah and Ramadi," the Major explained. "We will be helping to plan and coordinate infrastructure rebuilding projects and basic utility restoration, namely water and electric services. We will liaise with local tribal leaders and security forces to encourage them to join our efforts and not only contribute but lead by example and, if not in reality, at least superficially give the impression to the residents that local leaders and fellow Iraqis are taking charge in the rebuilding while the Americans are simply lending a hand and offering consulting services. We will also be compensating residents for material damages either directly or indirectly caused by U.S. military actions."

Major Warren finished briefing Fahdi on the unit's mission and introduced him to the members of the team, five Marine Sergeants all in their early-to mid-twenties.

Following the pleasantries, Fahdi's orders were to return to the Civil Affairs tent the following morning at 8 a.m. to join the team for breakfast and the Major's morning briefing, then they'd depart with an Army convoy for their first day of patrol at nine o'clock sharp.

Fahdi was excited by the fact he wouldn't have to get up at the crack of dawn. He liked his new job already.

During breakfast, Fahdi immediately learned the first rule of being a Marine: making fun of members of other branches of the U.S. military. Several of the members of Major Warren's Civil Affairs team took one look at Fahdi, dressed in his Army uniform, and curled their lips in disgust.

"Dude, what are you wearing?" one commented in a dramatically appalled tone.

"Who gave that to you?" another commented with equal revulsion.

Fahdi immediately froze, fearing perhaps the Marines weren't pleased to see an Iraqi in an American uniform.

"The EOD unit . . . I worked for before . . . they gave it to me," he stammered sheepishly. "They said I could wear it. They told me to wear it. Should I take it off?" Fahdi asked uneasily. He looked to Major Warren for guidance, but the Major remained focused on his breakfast and appeared indifferent to the current exchange underway between his Marines and Fahdi.

"If you're going to be out patrolling with us, you can't wear that faggoty shit."

"Relax man, they're just fucking with you," Sergeant Vallejo said without looking up from his pile of cold scrambled eggs. He was Major Warren's unofficial second-in-command and when he spoke, the other guys shut their mouths. "Give him a break," he added addressing his fellow Marines. "The poor guy's about to piss down his leg."

The group went silent and, at that, Major Warren finally looked up from his breakfast and smiled warmly at Fahdi. "We'll get you a set of Marine BDUs the next time we make a PX run over at TQ," he said casually, then addressed the group. "All right Marines, let's discuss today's mission."

In crisp unison, the Marines swiftly pushed their breakfast plates away and focused all attention on their Major.

"We are going to travel with an Army convoy out into the rural farmland area to the northeast of Camp Manhattan." He produced a military map of Iraq from his left chest pocket and flattened it out on the table. "This region here is mostly date farms," he said, drawing an invisible circle on the map with his finger. "We know they rely on pumping water from the Euphrates River to irrigate their crops," Warren said as he traced the blue line cutting its way through Western Iraq. "Since these pumps run on electricity and the power has been down since a few weeks after the invasion, these people are hurting. Some have managed to get ahold of generators, but most can't afford the black-market prices or can't even get to Baghdad to purchase one. We will start by going farm-to-farm to find out what they need to get their operations back up and running. Do they need generators? If so, what size and how many? How about the water pumps themselves? Have they been damaged? What parts do they need to repair them? Are there any other pertinent items or equipment they require to restore operational capacity to their business? Sergeant Vallejo and I will ask the questions. Fahdi will translate. Sergeant Ramirez will take notes. The rest of you will hold a close-range perimeter when we are engaging with any locals to ensure no insurgents run up behind us and fire a mortar up our ass. The Army will do their best to secure a large perimeter as we move between farms. Does everyone understand their mission for today?"

Warren's Marines all nodded confidently and erupted with a resounding, "Ooh-Rah Major!"

"Let's move out. Fahdi, you ride with me," the Major added as everyone stood up from the table.

Major Warren instructed one of his Marines to take Fahdi back to the team's tent to grab him some body armor and then the pair met up with the convoy at the main gate of the camp.

There were eight vehicles total in the convoy: six Army vehicles with a total of twenty to twenty-five soldiers and the six-man Marine Civil Affairs team divided into two Humvees.

The convoy pulled out and traveled northwest for several miles along a dirt road running parallel to the Euphrates. The convoy came to a stop and the Major announced, "We walk from here."

The team's radio man, Sergeant Santos, relayed the announcement to the Marines in the Humvee behind them. All scrambled from the vehicles and ensured their weapons were locked and loaded.

The Major turned to Fahdi. "Whenever we are out on a mission, you remain nut-to-butt with me. Do you understand?" Fahdi stared back blankly. Although he had an idea, he wasn't quite sure what "nut-to-butt" meant and hoped the Major would expound on his statement. "Stay behind me and don't let more than six inches get between us," Major Warren clarified, much to Fahdi's relief. "Also, Sergeant Juarez will serve as your de-facto bodyguard whenever we are out on patrol," the Major added. "You will be my shadow and Juarez will be yours."

Two of the Army soldiers slipped into the driver seats of the Marines' Humvees, and as the Civil Affairs Unit continued down the road on foot, the convoy slowly rolled along a short distance behind the team. The landscape was blanketed in date palm farms and dotted with farm houses approximately every quarter to half mile.

The team systematically moved house to house knocking on doors and talking to the residents.

"Major Warren was very polite, respectful, and constantly smiling. As is the custom in Iraq, the people would invite us in and the Major would always remove his helmet and body armor to show trust and try to break down the wall between the U.S. military and the locals. He knew what he was doing and was quite good at it. He asked the residents of each house we visited the same set of questions: How are they and their families doing in general? Do they have access to water and electricity? Do they need anything in specific to get their farms back up and running or keep them running? The first couple of days mainly revolved around reconnaissance and information collection, at least that's what I ascertained from what I was told and witnessed.

"All I knew for sure was we did a hell of a lot of walking. I was out of shape and, having been a heavy smoker for a few months at that point, I simply lacked the physical stamina needed to keep up with the Marines. I didn't want to slow them down and I sure as hell didn't want to look like a pussy, so I pushed myself to keep up. It was grueling."

At midday on the first day, Major Warren's team returned to the convoy for an MRE lunch break. Sergeant Ramirez pulled a case of MRE's from the back of the Humvee and began rummaging through the box. "Hey, uh, Fuh-dee, what kind of MRE you want? Beef or chicken?"

"I think his name is pronounced FAY-dee, numb-nuts," Sergeant Juarez corrected.

"You're both fucking idiots," Sergeant Goldberg announced. "It's FAH-dee."

"You need a new fucking name, dude," Ramirez suggested. "Something that's easier to say and remember. How about Fred?"

Fahdi looked from soldier to soldier, not super excited about being called Fred, but he really didn't have a say in what they called him anyway and didn't much care.

"No, not Fred. That's even worse than Fahdi," Juarez argued.

"You should have an alias though," Major Warren interjected. It's not safe for local terps to use their real names. How about Allen? You remind me of an Allen."

"I like Allen," Fahdi smiled. Anything was better than Fred, and he'd rather the Major gave him his name as opposed to the others.

From that day forward, Fahdi was known and referred to as Allen by the Marines on the Civil Affairs Unit and throughout Camp Manhattan. Major Warren even had "Allen" put on the uniform nametag of Fahdi's new set of Marine BDUs they picked up at the PX a few days later.

As the afternoon crept on and the Civil Affairs team approached what Major Warren had decided would be the last farmhouse they'd visit for the day, a barrage of mortars began to rain down in the field around the Marines.

"Take cover! Take cover!" Major Warren and Sergeant Vallejo screamed simultaneously.

Fahdi quickly surveyed the area for some type of shelter. But considering they were in the middle of an open field, he wasn't sure where he was supposed to "take cover." Before he could blink an eye, Sergeant Juarez grabbed Fahdi from the back of his body armor, threw him to the ground like a rag doll, and covered him with his own body. A couple more mortars fell from the sky, then silence.

The Marines stayed on the ground until they heard the

soldiers of the convoy parked up on the road begin returning rifle fire in the direction from which the mortars were launched.

As soon as Juarez climbed off, Fahdi scrambled to his feet.

"When the attack was over, I thought to myself, *Holy shit, this U.S. Marine just used his body to shield me, a local Iraqi, from mortars being fired by other Iraqis.* Even though he'd been ordered to do so in the chaos of battle, he could have simply dropped beside me and no one would have faulted him for it. These guys were unlike any U.S. military personnel I'd ever worked with before, they were amazing. I instantly developed a profound respect for those guys."

No one was injured in the attack. Thankfully, whoever fired the mortars had a bad aim.

A few minutes later, a U.S. Army chopper arrived overhead. The convoy had radioed for air support immediately upon being attacked. Fahdi figured they'd pack it in and head back to base, but Major Warren had other plans. The Marines got up, brushed themselves off, and continued their mission.

The Civil Affairs team cautiously made their way to the farmhouse while the convoy sent a team of ten soldiers to locate the position from which the mortar attack was launched to gather evidence.

"Every time we were fired on, it was as if we'd been attacked by ghosts. Trying to hunt down the perpetrators, the most we ever found was simple stuff like spent AK rounds, sometimes a mortar tube, or an RPG launcher they could not carry away quickly, but never any actual insurgents. They'd just fucking vanish into thin air."

Major Warren finally gave the order to return to camp as light began to fade.

As everyone exited the vehicles and gathered their equipment, Warren told Fahdi to grab a shower and meet the team at the chow hall in an hour.

"Are we having a meeting?" Fahdi asked.

"No," Warren answered.

"Do I need to bring anything?" Fahdi inquired, somewhat confused. "Should I wear my uniform?"

"No and no. What's with the twenty questions?"

"Well, I was just wondering why we're meeting back up."

"To have dinner," Warren stated matter-of-factly. "You *do* eat dinner, don't you?"

"O-oh, well, y-yes," Fahdi sputtered. "I guess I'll see you guys in an hour."

Fahdi had never been invited by any of the units he'd served with to join them for a meal unless there was a specific reason for him to be there such as a meeting, a debriefing, etc. Fahdi assumed the only reason he'd been invited to join them for breakfast was to be present for the Major's morning briefing. Fahdi soon learned Major Warren was adamant about his team, including Fahdi, dining together as a "family" for all meals. He felt it helped them bond and was an ideal way to decompress tensions and anxieties.

The only clothes Fahdi had, aside from his uniform, was a pair of jeans. Scrambling into them after his shower, he left to meet the team at the chow hall. Even though it was only late March, the weather had heated up significantly in this area of Iraq. Jeans were a little hot to be roaming around in, but Fahdi didn't have the option of running to his house to grab cooler clothing. Joining the Marines at their table in the chow hall, all were dressed in their PT shorts and t-shirts.

"Dude, aren't you hot?" Sergeant Juarez said as Fahdi sat down. "It's hot as balls! How can you stand wearing jeans? Don't you have any shorts?"

"And why do you look like you just stepped out of a 1980's *Wham!* video?" Sergeant Ramirez joshed. "What's with the acid wash?"

Fahdi was already aware the style of jeans currently popular in Iraq was considered far outdated by American standards. Sergeant Benning and the other drill sergeants back in Ramadi had made fun of Fahdi's and the other Iraqi locals' clothing styles on numerous occasions. This was nothing new for Fahdi. "Well, I don't have any shorts. It's either this or my uniform," Fahdi responded.

"The next time you go home pick up some shorts, man," Juarez said.

"Sure, you want to give me ride to my house in Baghdad?" Fahdi asked facetiously. "Cuz the only way I'm leaving this base is with a U.S. military convoy or escort or I'll end up dead in a ditch somewhere."

Before anyone could say anything else, the Major changed the subject. "So, Allen, what do you think about the people we talked to today? Do you think they will be willing to work with the Americans to help rebuild and push out the insurgency, or are they still afraid of us?"

"Well, they're not really afraid *of* you, they're afraid of being *seen* with you," Fahdi answered. "For the most part, they want your help and they want to work with the Americans, but they know if the wrong people see them cooperating with you, they and their entire families will be killed. Especially since the Americans don't have a very good track record in the area of being able to protect the locals from the insurgency."

The Major nodded and returned his attention to his dinner. Fahdi wondered if he'd been a little too candid in his response but figured Warren wanted the truth.

After dinner, Sergeant Vallejo invited Fahdi to come back to their tent with them to watch some DVDs. The team was taking the next day off and planned to indulge in a "movie night" to unwind.

Dinner and a movie! Fahdi was elated!

The team had a small TV, DVD player, and PlayStation in their tent. Fahdi hung out with the Marines until well past midnight playing video games, watching movies, and shooting-the-shit.

The next morning, Major Warren and a couple of the guys took Fahdi on a shopping spree over at the PX on TQ Air Base. They got him a set of Marine BDUs, new boots, and even a couple of pairs of Marine PT shorts. Fahdi had been proud to wear the Army uniform, but felt truly honored to be given the privilege of donning the Marine uniform.

"Working with Major Warren and his unit was a real turning point for me. For the first time, I had friends inside an American base, real 'buddies' who made me feel like I was part of a team. Until then, I always felt like a hired hand, an 'outsider.' I'd started getting a little closer with Sergeant Benning back at the ICDC boot camp in Ramadi, but it was nothing like the relationship I had with the Marine Civil Affairs guys, and I don't think it ever would have developed into anything like that even if I'd have worked with Benning for a year. Major Warren not only took me in as a fellow Marine, a brother, he valued my input, listened to my suggestions, and respected my opinions."

The following day, the Civil Affairs team and their Army escorts headed out for another day of door knocking in one of the rural farm areas. The convoy was traveling their usual route along the river when suddenly Fahdi heard a familiar BOOM! *Son-of-a-bitch! An IED!*

All the vehicles in the convoy came to a screeching halt and everyone jumped out with their weapons drawn in preparation to retaliate. But as usual, there were no enemy combatants in sight. The Humvee two vehicles behind Fahdi's had taken a direct hit from the IED. Both Civil Affairs Humvees had rolled right over it. Major Warren ran back to assist the men in the smoldering Humvee while the other Marines joined the soldiers in securing a perimeter around the convoy. Fahdi was ordered to remain in the vehicle.

There were five men in the targeted Humvee; the soldier in the front passenger seat was killed instantly, the other four were seriously injured.

The Major returned to the Humvee with an entirely new demeanor. He'd pocketed his Civil Affairs face and put on his war face. The other Marines on the team transformed as well, like someone had flipped a switch.

"Out of the Humvee, Allen," Major Warren said in a sharp, commanding tone. "We're going door knocking."

The Major knew whoever had detonated the IED had to be close, and since it was such a sparsely populated area with few structures, there weren't many places to hide. The culprit or culprits were either crouched in a field somewhere nearby or hiding out in one of the few farmhouses in the immediate vicinity. The team jogged to the nearest house. But when they got to the door, they didn't knock, they kicked it in. Fahdi entered the house behind the team, prepared to translate for the Major, but Major Warren wasn't smiling or asking any questions today. Without saying a word, he made it perfectly clear to the occupants of the house they were to sit down and shut up while his men swept the house looking for evidence of a trigger or hostiles.

"We spent the morning jumping fences, breaking into outbuildings, rummaging through sheds, and systematically going from farm to farm looking for anyone or anything suspicious. The Army had dispatched their own search party to do the same thing we were doing but headed in the opposite direction.

By the end of the morning, both the Civil Affairs Marines and the Army had rounded up about twenty young guys and were holding them near the convoy. They searched them all for any sort of signaling devices that could have been used to detonate the IED, but came up empty-handed. Major Warren had me translate as he questioned them, but it was always the same story: nobody saw, heard, or knew anything. By the end of the morning, since we'd come up with jack shit, the Major had to let them all go."

That evening, Fahdi decided to wear his new Marine PT shorts to the chow hall for his usual "dinner date" with the Civil Affairs team. Fahdi noticed the guys typically wore sneakers with their shorts, but Fahdi had forgotten to buy a pair while at the PX over at TQ. All he had were his uniform boots, a pair of flip flops, and his old beat-up pair of civilian loafers he'd come from Baghdad with. He decided the best option would be to stick with the marine-issued boots.

Big mistake.

As soon the Civil Affairs Unit caught sight of Fahdi approaching the table in his little PT shorts and boots laced up into a perfect bow, the entire team erupted into hysterical laughter.

Fahdi froze.

"Dude, no!" Sergeant Juarez managed to sputter between gasps of uncontrollable cackling.

"What now?" Fahdi asked looking down, flustered.

"Oh, my God, man, you're totally hopeless," Juarez remarked, tossing his head back and forth.

"Perhaps we should make another run to the PX to pick you

up some tennis shoes," Major Warren said, doing his best to suppress a smirk himself.

When lunchtime rolled around the next day, Major Warren directed the convoy to TQ Air Base to give the guys a real meal at TQ's massive chow hall and Fahdi the opportunity to run by the PX to pick up some sneakers.

As the sun set, the team invited Fahdi to another "movie night" at their tent to watch *Black Hawk Down*. When the movie was over, one of the guys turned to Fahdi and asked, "So what did ya think man? Did you like the movie?"

"Yes, it was good," Fahdi responded. "I just don't understand how you guys can be living literally on a battlefield fighting a war every day yourselves and still watch war movies in your time off. Don't you need a break? Maybe watch a fucking Disney movie every now and then or something?"

Before anyone could say anything else, the distant sound of the day's final call to prayer echoed from one of the Mosques on the outskirts of Habbaniyah. The whole tent grew quiet and remained silent throughout the first several seconds of the Mullah's chanting refrain over the loudspeaker.

Finally, Sergeant Santos broke the silence, "Hey Allen, how come you're not praying?"

"Yeah, man," Sergeant Juarez piped in, "we always see other terps and locals who work on base stopping for prayers throughout the day. How come we never see you do it?"

Fahdi hadn't realized, until that moment, everyone assumed he was Muslim, but it's not like it wasn't a fair assumption.

"Well, you don't see me praying because I'm not Muslim," Fahdi answered plainly.

"What?" Vallejo asked with a shocked look, an expression most of the Marines in the tent now shared.

"Then what *are* you?" Juarez asked as if it were now possible Fahdi was some form of intergalactic alien.

"I'm Christian," Fahdi answered.

"Christian? Like, what, Baptist or something?" Ramirez asked.

"No, I'm Catholic."

"What? They got Catholics in Iraq?" Juarez practically shrieked. "That's awesome man. We're all Catholic, too. Well, except for Goldberg over there. He's a cheap Jew, but we don't hold it against him," Juarez jabbed.

Goldberg flipped Juarez the bird. "Suck my balls, dickhead."

"Oh, man, I can't wait to tell the Major you're Catholic," Vallejo said almost giddily. "He totally thinks you're a Muslim."

Major Warren had taken a call on his satellite phone sometime around the middle of the movie and had stepped outside the tent to conduct his conversation. A few minutes later, a couple of the guys heard him walk off and he had yet to return. It wasn't unusual for the Major to slip off to Headquarters at odd hours to take care of officer duties.

"Did you convert to Christianity?" Ramirez asked Fahdi.

"No, I was born Christian. You don't get to pick your religion here in Iraq. You're stuck with whatever you're born into. My entire family is Christian."

"Has your family always been Christian?" Vallejo asked.

"Well, according to records in our Church in Northern Iraq, my family's been Christian since at least the early 9th Century."

"Holy shit! You could be directly related to Jesus or some shit!" Juarez exclaimed, only half-joking.

"Um, I don't think so," Fahdi replied, shaking his head.

Right then, Major Warren reappeared in the tent. One look at the Major's stony glare and everyone knew something was very wrong. Fahdi immediately recognized the expression—war face. The Major had just learned of the gruesome deaths of four Blackwater contractors who'd been murdered earlier that day and whose burned and mutilated bodies were hanging from a steel bridge in Fallujah, a mere ten miles down the road from Camp Manhattan.

CHAPTER NINE

FALLUJAH GETS LIT UP

APRIL 2004

After the brutal deaths of the Blackwater contractors, the mood within the Civil Affairs team, and the atmosphere throughout the entire camp for that matter, was somber and determined.

"Everyone was on edge. You could cut the tension with a knife," Fahdi, recalled, taking a drag of his umpteenth cigarette.

On April 4, 2004, in response to the murders of the Blackwater contractors, U.S. forces launched Operation Vigilant Resolve, also referred to as the First Battle of Fallujah.

Leading up to the campaign, the U.S. Army set up an armed perimeter around the city and established checkpoints at various entry and exit points. The Euphrates formed a natural barrier around part of the city and the Army set up check points at each of the bridges crossing the river. Major Warren's team spent the first two weeks of April camped out at a checkpoint on the far side of the bridge that deposited travelers onto the main road leading west to Ramadi. Their mission was to interview the people coming across the bridge as they fled the chaos inside Fallujah to ensure they were legitimate civilian residents and not foreign fighters attempting to escape.

"We didn't move from the end of that damn bridge for ten straight days. We lived off MREs and slept in the Humvees. I swear Major Warren didn't sleep at all the entire time. I never saw the man close his eyes once. We passed out MREs and water to the people coming across the bridge as a gesture of goodwill and as a non-confrontational way to get them to stop and talk to us. Instead of shoving a gun in their face and asking questions, we handed out food and asked questions. It was also a good way to screen people. If anyone coming out of Fallujah turned down free food and water, it was a serious red flag.

As soon as Warren's team had the residents stopped and talking, one of the first things Fahdi tried to hone in on was their accent. Being a native Iraqi gave him an advantage over many of the other translators who, although native Arabic speakers, were from a variety of countries throughout the Middle East. Fahdi was able to pick right up on a foreign accent or even someone faking an Iraqi accent. Whereas other linguists had a lot more difficulty distinguishing one accent from another. For example: Saudi Arabian and Iraqi accents are similar. An Egyptian or Lebanese translator would struggle to differentiate between the two. The U.S. military tried to bring in as many local transla-tors as possible for the Fallujah battle, hoping to have several stationed at each of the checkpoints exiting the city, but the day the operation started, most of the local Iraqi interpreters quit and returned home.

"I was one of the few locals who stuck around," Fahdi said later. "And, no, it wasn't because I was courageous and noble. It was because I was young and dumb. I was totally clueless of how hard the shit was about to hit the fan. I know the U.S. received a lot of criticism over the way they handled the Fallujah situation. I couldn't even begin to confirm or deny the many atrocities the U.S. military was accused of committing during that battle, but I can attest to what I personally witnessed. I watched numerous families leave Fallujah under relatively peaceful conditions. The Army went to great lengths to warn the population, too great in my opinion. They gave the citizens ample time and opportunity to leave Fallujah, but this also opened a window for a lot of insurgents to escape as well. The Americans did what they could to virtually seal off the city, but it was impossible to fortify every inch of the entire perimeter. The Army posted and distributed flyers across the city, warning the people of the impending attack. For two days, they had the mosques broadcasting warnings over their loudspeakers advising people to leave. Hell, I even heard the announcements from where I was on the far side of the river. The people in Fallujah could clearly see the colossal American forces amassing around their city. I have no idea what would have possessed any of them, especially families with children, to remain.

"My theory is a lot of the civilians who got caught up in the city when the U.S. launched their attack were either threatened and essentially forced at gunpoint by the insurgents to stay in the city to serve as human shields or were murdered before the U.S. even arrived, simply for propaganda purposes. I'm sure the U.S. troops made mistakes and killed civilians, but not nearly on the scale they've been accused.

"On the bright side, it was during our stay at the bridge that I finally learned how to pee in a bottle," Fahdi proudly added. "All the other guys had been doing their business in empty plastic bottles while I continued to hike off into the desert in an attempt to find some privacy doing mine. A couple of days into our stay,

I was out in the middle of nowhere taking a pee break when we came under attack. Insurgents from inside Fallujah began lobbing mortars and firing at us from across the river. I heard the guys on our side begin returning fire and I suddenly thought to myself, *Son-of-a-bitch! I'm going to die out here all alone with my dick hanging out!* I half-ran, half-hobbled back to the checkpoint with my pants undone, practically around my knees, and took cover with a couple of the other guys behind one of the team's Humvees. Within a few minutes, the attack was over and, thankfully, no one on our side had been injured. Major Warren said it probably had been blind fire from a group of desperate fighters trying to shoot their way out of the city, or an attempt to cause some distraction while others tried to sneak out."

Fahdi buttoned up his BDU pants while Sergeant Vallejo seized the opportunity to chide him for his distant "bathroom hikes."

"Allen, why are you going all the way out there to take a piss?" Vallejo probed. "Just pee in a damn bottle, dude."

"I want some privacy," Fahdi retorted.

"What are you so embarrassed about? Is your junk small or something?" Juarez teased.

Fahdi rolled his eyes. But before he could respond, Major Warren was looming over him, holding an empty water bottle. "This is your toilet now," the Major said sternly as he thrust the bottle into Fahdi's chest. "I don't want you more than ten yards away from me outside of camp. Do you understand?"

"Yes, sir," Fahdi replied sheepishly.

The following day the Marine infantry swarmed into Fallujah, initiating the primary brunt of the U.S. campaign to retake control of the city.

"It was total insanity . . ." Fahdi closed his eyes, struggling to find the words to describe what unfolded in Fallujah, what will be forever fresh in his mind. "I wasn't even in the city. I was clear on the other side of the river and couldn't believe what was happening. It was complete chaos. So loud . . . and nonstop fighting. We heard AK-47s, M-16s, M-4s, RPGs, .50 cals, and endless small arms fire. The Marines literally lit the entire place up. We watched it glow like a fucking roman candle for two days.

"I could tell the guys on the team felt like they should have been there, in the city, with their fellow Marines. They felt helpless. Major Warren kept telling everyone how they were doing more to help their brothers and their country by being right where they were, carrying out their mission as a Civil Affairs Unit, but I think he was saying it more to convince himself than his men. You could see it in his eyes. It took everything in him to keep from marching across that bridge and into the city to help."

By the tenth day of the Fallujah stakeout, the bulk of the combat operations were winding down and Major Warren decided it was time for the team to return to Camp Manhattan for a few hours to grab showers, eat some real food, and restock their MRE and water supply.

"We'd been getting by with baby wipes and they weren't cutting it anymore. We were all in desperate need of a real shower. Most of the guys had at least brought toothbrushes and razors to shave every day while we were away, but I hadn't shaved since we left the camp. After a week, the guys were making fun of me. My beard had started growing in and I looked like a 'terrorist.'

"Even though I took a lot of shit from the guys during those few weeks outside Fallujah, I realized it meant they were accepting me into their inner circle. They all started addressing me as Allen, whereas up to that point I was simply 'the terp.' It was always, 'Oh, *the terp* is here' '*The terp* is gone.' 'Ask *the terp* to do this . . .' 'Tell *the terp* to do that . . .' So instead of being just 'the terp,' I was now Allen and part of the team."

As the operation moved into its third week, the flow of civilians coming out of Fallujah slowed to a trickle. At that point, those who hadn't left yet were better off staying put and barricading themselves in their homes rather than trying to move about the streets. The Civil Affairs team went from having long lines of people to question as they tried to come through the check point, to having quite a bit of downtime.

"We had nothing better to do than sit around and talk. I quickly discovered Marines in a warzone talk primarily about two subjects: 1) killing people, and 2) sex. They talked about their girlfriends, compared how many girls they'd slept with, and tried to one-up each other with stories of their various sexual escapades. Unsurprisingly, I thought it was awesome, quite entertaining, that is until they started interrogating me. They asked me how many girls I'd been with and how old I was when I lost my virginity. Sex is a subject Iraqis don't discuss, even young guys just hanging out together, it's strictly taboo. And, you definitely don't talk about it if you aren't married, because you're not supposed to be doing it. Openly admitting to having sex before marriage in Iraq is like admitting to committing a serious crime, and it's never smart to incriminate yourself, even with your friends. Therefore, I lied, and told them I'd never been with a girl. Boy, was that a mistake."

"What?" Sergeant Santos screeched. "You've never had sex?"

"Have you ever seen a girl naked?" Sergeant Ramirez pressed.

"Do you even know what a pussy looks like, dude?" Sergeant Santos asked.

"You see Goldberg over there," Juarez said pointing to the team Medic standing a few yards away smoking a cigarette, "that's what a pussy looks like."

"Kiss my ass, fuck stick," Goldberg replied.

The group burst into laughter that was a little too loud and prompted a disapproving glare from Major Warren.

"Poor Goldberg was always getting picked on," Fahdi smirked, shaking his head, "but I think it was a defense mechanism that stemmed from Goldberg being the team medic. All the guys on the team knew he'd seen them cry at one point in time. Marines don't like to be vulnerable. Goldberg took their shit like a champ, and he was also the one who held them in his arms when they were bleeding and screaming in pain, which he also handled like a champ. Fortunately for Goldberg, I now absorbed some of the incessant torment he typically had to endure alone. Needless to say, I was teased relentlessly about my lack of sexual experience from that day forward, but all in good fun. As a matter of fact, everything was a joke to those guys. I swear, one minute they could be in the middle of a firefight with insurgents, dodging RPGs and mortars, and thirty seconds later they'd be back to making fun of each other and cracking jokes. I didn't know if they were just super laid back guys or completely insane. Looking back, I'd say it was a little bit of both."

As Operation Vigilant Resolve wound down toward the end of April 2004, the U.S. military went to work questioning the approximately 1,200 suspected insurgents they'd rounded up during the battle. Due to the vast number of detainees and the high number of local translators who vanished during the conflict, the Army was critically short on linguists to assist the American interrogators in questioning the captives.

The Civil Affairs team had completed their assignment at the Fallujah bridge checkpoint and were preparing to resume their original mission when Major Warren was asked (politely forced) to loan Fahdi to the Army for a few days to assist with the interrogations until another batch of translators could be brought in from Baghdad. The Major informed Fahdi, who then feared he'd be transferred permanently.

"I was sure I'd never see the guys on the Civil Affairs team again, which seriously bummed me out. I begged the Major to talk them out of using me. He promised it would only be for a few days, and said he'd make sure I was reassigned to his unit once the new terp reinforcements arrived. I wasn't convinced, but there was no fighting it."

Fahdi reported to the make-shift detention facility on Camp Manhattan at 8 a.m. the following morning and asked for a Chief Warrant Officer Stanley, who Major Warren had told Fahdi he'd be working for. CWO Stanley showed up and asked Fahdi where his DOD badge was.

"Excuse me, sir? My what?" Fahdi questioned, confused.

"Your Department of Defense badge," the CWO reiterated in a frustrated tone. "You are my translator, right? I'm assuming you do speak English?"

"Yes, sir, I do . . . I mean, I speak English," Fahdi stumbled. "But I don't have a DOD badge, sir. I have a Titan badge." Fahdi produced his Titan employee badge and handed it to the Warrant Officer.

"You're a goddamn local?" the CWO exclaimed with genuine surprise. "I can't use a local. The translator for this position is required to have a security clearance, or at least be a U.S. resident."

"I guess you guys are desperate," Fahdi replied with half a smile, trying to break the ice a little. "I heard a new batch of translators is supposed to be arriving in a few days. I'll go back to my other unit if you can't use me."

Fahdi tried not to appear too excited as he attempted to wriggle his way out of the job.

"No, there's no time," Stanley replied with ire. "We have to release a lot of these assholes in seventy-two hours unless we can come up with something more to hold them on. You'll have to do."

Fahdi followed Stanley down a narrow hallway. They passed several doors with armed soldiers posted beside them. Stanley halted before one of the doors and the guard told Fahdi to empty his pockets. Fahdi did as instructed and promptly had his cigarettes and lighter confiscated. The guard then gave Fahdi a full-body pat down, even had him remove his shoes and socks. Satisfied Fahdi was clean of any weapons or contraband, he gave CWO Stanley the go ahead to enter.

Fahdi followed Stanley into a tiny windowless room containing three metal folding chairs and a small table. Seated in one of the folding chairs was a young Iraqi man, chained to the table.

"You, sit here and don't move," Stanley barked as he shoved Fahdi down into one of the chairs. "Say exactly what I say, when I say it, and how I say it."

Gee, that sounds familiar.

"Then you tell me exactly what this asshole says back. You don't add anything, you don't change anything, and you don't share any of your opinions. You do not analyze. You merely translate everything word-for-word. Do you understand?"

"Yes, sir.

"I was scared shitless. I think I was more nervous than the guy chained to the table. I was used to being ordered around and shouted at after working with the drill instructors, but if you pissed them off, the worst they could do was make you run or do pushups. If I fucked up and pissed this guy off, I was afraid he'd ship my ass off to Abu Ghraib."

Fahdi and CWO Stanley spent the next seventy-two hours

working round-the-clock interrogating four different captives in various intervals.

"We'd typically spend an hour or two talking to a detainee, then we'd take a thirty-minute break before moving on to questioning the next. A couple of times, Stanley grilled a guy for six or even eight hours straight. They weren't allowed to have water or bathroom breaks during the interrogation, but we didn't get any either. So, however long Stanley could go without water or peeing was how long the detainee and I would have to last, too. Stanley even conducted interview sessions in the middle of the night. On the second and third days, I left the detention facility around 8 p.m. and Stanley told me to be back at 2 a.m. They'd drag the detainees out of bed and haul them in for interrogation, hoping that in their exhausted stupor they'd slip up and admit to something or say something useful.

"I absolutely hated it. That assignment was even worse than working with the EOD guys. We'd sit with a detainee and ask the same question over and over and over again. Sometimes Stanley would ask the same question in different ways; sometimes he'd literally repeat the exact same question for an hour. It was mind-numbing. Hell, sometimes it got to the point where *I* was ready to confess! 'Fuck it, it was me! Can we please just get out of this room now?'

"Predictably the detainees' responses were always the same: 'It wasn't me.' 'I didn't do anything.' 'I don't know anything.' 'I didn't see anything.' 'They came into my house and arrested me for no reason.' 'I'm innocent.' And throughout it all, the Chief would repeat the same song and dance: 'Lying isn't going to help you. If you tell us something useful or give us names of people, we might let you go or cut you a deal.' And, of course, we'd ask them all the golden question, 'Do you know where Zarqawi is hiding?' (Abu Musab al-Zarqawi, the key insurgency leader in Iraq from 2004 to 2006.) Asking one of the detainees this question, he literally said, 'Who?' He genuinely had no fucking clue who Zarqawi even was.

"The whole thing was such a fucking waste of time. Three solid days. The same question, the same answers. They all knew the Americans weren't going to torture them. They weren't even scared. The Chief would yell, scream, cuss, and even bang his fist on the table, but never laid a finger on any of the detainees. In the end, we got nowhere. In my humble opinion, two of the four guys we drilled were completely clueless. They'd likely just been in the wrong place, at the wrong time, and had gotten caught up in a U.S. military sweep. Yet, I felt the other two were hiding something, holding back, but there was no way any amount of 'questioning' was going to get it out of them."

On top of everything else, Fahdi spent all day, every day, fiending for a cigarette. Obviously, there was no smoking in the interrogation room, but he wasn't even allowed to smoke during breaks between interrogation sessions as there was strictly no smoking allowed anywhere near the detention facility. Fahdi kept telling himself it was only three days, then he'd be back with the Civil Affairs team.

But as luck would have it, Stanley managed to present enough evidence to hold the two shady detainees longer than seventy-two hours. On the third day of Fahdi's interrogation duty, Stanley informed him during lunch that the new translators hadn't arrived yet from Baghdad and Fahdi would "get" to continue working with him into the following week. It took everything in Fahdi not to burst into tears.

Major Warren paid a visit to Fahdi's trailer later in the evening to say hello and check in on him. He, too, had been informed earlier in the day that Fahdi's assignment at the detention facility had been extended. He found Fahdi sitting on the ground outside his trailer smoking a cigarette.

"I know I can't ask you anything about what they've got you doing over there," the Major said with a smile. "I just wanted to stop by and see how you're doing and let you know the guys miss not seeing you around."

"I'm ready to shoot myself in the fucking face," Fahdi replied gloomily between long drags on his cigarette.

"Is it really that bad?"

"I don't have the patience for this shit. The dude asks the same fucking question ten million times. It would probably be quicker and a hell of a lot less frustrating for me to teach the detainee English or Stanley Arabic so they can talk to each other and leave me the hell out of it. Is there really nothing you can do to get me out of there?" Fahdi pleaded.

"Getting you out of there isn't only above my paygrade, it's on a completely different universal plane," Major Warren replied with a chuckle.

Fortuitously, Fahdi was only stuck on interrogation duty for a week. The new translators finally arrived and Fahdi was relieved of his post and granted approval to return to work for Major Warren. As soon as he was cut loose from the detention facility, Fahdi cheerfully made a beeline for the Civil Affairs tent to relay the good news to the Major.

"You might be jumping from the frying pan into the fire," Major Warren commented as Fahdi informed him he'd been granted permission to return to work for the Civil Affairs team. "Our new area of operations is now Fallujah. As soon as they officially declare Operation Vigilant Resolve over, HQ wants us to start pushing into Fallujah running relief and reconstruction missions."

"When do we get started?" Fahdi replied without batting an eye. "I'll happily walk straight through the middle of Fallujah in my damn underwear if it means I never have to go back to interrogating detainees."

"Well, let's hope it doesn't come to that, for our sake," Warren kidded. "On a serious note, though, I need you to meet us here at the tent tomorrow morning at 8 a.m. We're going over to the weapons range and I'd like you to join us."

"Will I get to shoot, too?" Fahdi said half-joking. He hadn't been allowed to touch a weapon since leaving Ramadi.

"Believe it or not, yes," the Major replied with a smile. "Considering how hot the area is right now, it's going to be all-hands-on-deck pushing forward into Fallujah. If shit hits the fan while we're out and about, you'll be more of an asset than a liability if you can shoot back. That is, of course, if you know your way around a rifle, which is what we're going to find out tomorrow at the range. It's not going to help us much if you accidentally shoot yourself in the foot, or one of us. Are you more comfortable with an M-16 or should I track down an AK for you?"

"I know how to use both, sir, but I'm more experienced with an AK."

Major Warren nodded. "AK, it is."

Fahdi and the Civil Affairs team spent the following morning on the TQ weapons range. Major Warren managed to borrow an AK-47 from an Iraqi Army unit stationed at TQ for Fahdi to practice with. He also let Fahdi shoot his .9mm.

Done at the range, the Major didn't clearly express to Fahdi whether or not he was satisfied with his weapon handling skills, and Fahdi was too shy to ask. He just hoped he'd proven himself enough to earn the privilege of carrying a weapon outside the base. Obviously, he would feel a lot safer having the ability to defend himself should the shit hit the fan, but it would also help him blend in as he interacted with the locals while out on missions. Being the only unarmed member of the team made him stick out like a sore thumb. Many locals viewed the Iraqis who served as translators for the U.S. as traitors and held even more animosity toward the translators than the U.S. troops themselves. As far as the locals were aware, terps were never armed. If Fahdi could walk in with a weapon, it would help prevent a lot of uncomfortable gazes and possible issues.

Fahdi later learned the Major was not only satisfied with his shooting skills but was quite impressed. He didn't voice this to Fahdi at the range because he wanted to discuss his plan to give Fahdi a weapon during missions with the rest of the team first; he wanted to ensure every Marine on his team was not only comfortable with Fahdi being armed but fully supported the Major's decision.

As they gathered to embark on their first day back out following the Battle of Fallujah, Fahdi started to climb into his usual spot in Major Warren's Humvee and found an AK-47 on the seat. All the guys on the Civil Affairs team had wholeheartedly given their blessing.

"The decision was unanimous," Major Warren said as Fahdi stared in disbelief. "You are our brother and we trust you to have our back just as we'll have yours. There's just one rule: you don't shoot unless you plan to kill."

CHAPTER TEN

SHORT-LIVED VICTORIES

MAY 2004

By mid-May, the Civil Affairs team had set up an outpost in one of the neighborhood Town Council buildings on the outskirts of Fallujah. Major Warren met with the eight Town Council members, which included a few Sheiks, a couple of prominent, local business owners, and other respected members of the local community. He instructed them to begin gathering information on area residents who'd suffered significant private property damage as a result of the recent U.S. military actions in the area. The Major and the Council members agreed on set indemnities for a variety of residential damages such as broken windows, busted doors, bullet holes, downed fences, damaged vehicles, etc. The Civil Affairs team then held a week-long "open claims" period during which residents could come to the City Council building, present physical or photographic evidence for the team to review, and receive cash compensation for any covered damages.

"Sergeant Ramirez was responsible for the 'cash bag. We went to the City Council building every day for a week with a military backpack stuffed with money, wads of hundred-dollar bills. The people would stand in line all day and, when it was finally their turn, they'd show Major Warren some grainy cell phone pictures while reciting the same sob story the dozens of others who were in line ahead of them just told. The Major would write a voucher the claimant would present to Sergeant Ramirez who'd reach into the cash bag and hand over whatever amount Major Warren specified. I have no idea how much money was in the bag. I just remember, whenever Sergeant Ramirez had it, he transformed into a completely different guy. He wouldn't look at or engage with anyone, not even the other guys on our own team. He'd only speak to the Major and only if the Major asked him a question. He wouldn't have even answered to God."

Major Warren's team was one of many dispatched in and around Fallujah to conduct reparations missions in the wake of Operation Vigilant Resolve. Cash was literally being dumped into the city and a lot of it was not used to patch bullet holes or fix broken windows. A bulk of the money found its way into the hands of the insurgency who used it to help finance their operations. Sadly, over the next several years, American troops would be killed and maimed by IEDs and other weapons built and purchased with the very money the U.S. military handed over to the citizens of Al-Anbar province in the months after the Battle of Fallujah.

Once they had completed their reparations assignment in Fallujah, the Civil Affairs team resumed their original mission of assisting rural residents in rebuilding and reconstruction efforts to get their farms back up and running.

Major Warren designed a small brochure outlining his team's services, had Fahdi translate it into Arabic, and then had a few hundred printed off at one of the Army offices on TQ Air Base. They began distributing the brochures to residents of a small village twenty minutes north of Fallujah.

Right before breaking for lunch on their first day in the village, the team visited the home of a local Sheikh who was eager to assist the Major in his efforts to help the local populace. The Sheikh and the team spent an entire afternoon discussing the current conditions and immediate issues needing to be addressed, then the Sheikh offered to accompany the team as they performed their door-to-door visits. The Major ensured the Sheikh understood the risks of being seen actively assisting a U.S. military unit in the area, telling him about several recent civilians who'd been brutally murdered by the insurgency as reprisal for helping the American forces, but the Sheikh was not deterred and declared his adamancy to do whatever it took to help the people of his village.

"The Sheikh was a really nice man and having him with us as we visited the locals helped eliminate the fear typically roused by a bunch of armed Marines suddenly showing up on their doorstep. It made it so much easier for us to get them to open up to us. It would usually take the Major twenty minutes to get five words out of a farmer, whereas the Sheikh would have him singing his entire life story to us in two minutes.

"The primary issue the village faced was lack of electricity. They hadn't had power since the war had ended a little over a year ago. Major Warren arranged to have several generators delivered and hooked up throughout the village. He also had an Army combat engineer unit from TQ Air Base come out and help hook them up and make minor infrastructure repairs. The Major really went out of his way to help the village and wanted people to realize the U.S. wasn't just in their country to fight and destroy, they were also there to rebuild and try to give them a better life.

"Around the end of May, the Major felt we'd done all we could to help that particular village and it was time to move on. The Sheikh was thankful for all we had done and asked us to stay, but understood we had to go."

On the team's final day in the village, a lot of the residents came out to greet them and wish them well, smiling and waving from their homes or standing roadside as the convoy passed by on its way back to base.

"It was the first time we felt like we'd accomplished something, like we'd made a real difference. The guys on the team had started to get a little depressed and were feeling kind of useless, considering they'd been on the ground in Iraq for two months and had accomplished very little. Plus, being forced to stand on the sidelines during the Battle of Fallujah really bummed them out, so this accomplishment was just as much a moral triumph for them as it was a benefit for the people of the village."

Any form of victory in Iraq was, regrettably, short-lived. As the Civil Affairs team and their Army escorts made their way back to the base, the convoy took a direct hit from a devastating IED.

"It was the worst IED attack we'd suffered so far; actually, the worst one I've ever experienced in my entire life," Fahdi said as he lit a cigarette and assumed a thousand-yard stare out into the darkness. "Again, though, the Civil Affairs team and I were lucky. We were three vehicles back from the Humvee that took the brunt of the explosion. The five soldiers inside were just . . . gone. They had no chance. The blast was so intense it even injured a couple of the soldiers in the Humvees in front of and behind the one obliterated.

"What made this IED so effective was that, unlike most IEDs, it wasn't buried or laying on the side of the road, it was strapped to a tree several feet off the ground, about level with the Humvees as they passed. The entire area was a giant palm farm; the sides of the road and median were lined with trees. Everyone was constantly scanning for IEDs, and EOD units had probably even been up and down that road sometime in the last twenty-four hours, but everyone was focused on the ground, no one considered looking for one suspended from a damn tree."

After the blast, the remaining vehicles in the convoy parked in a zigzag pattern to block the road and everyone jumped out. As usual, there was a bout of arbitrary gunfire in random directions. The only structure within site was a small ice factory and one of the soldiers called out he saw someone duck into the building after the explosion.

Since Major Warren was the highest-ranking officer in the convoy, he took charge of assembling a team to go in and search the ice factory. The Major instructed the soldiers in the convoy, who weren't tending to the wounded, to surround the building while he led a team of seven—with Fahdi in tow—into the factory. For the first time since beginning to carry a weapon while out on rounds, Fahdi switched the safety off and held his AK in an offensive position.

Before entering the factory, Major Warren cautioned Fahdi, "If we end up in a firefight, do your best to gain a visual on who is shooting and shoot back. And try to make sure the person you're shooting at is armed before you open fire."

Major Warren had already violated quite a few regulations and rules of engagement by allowing Fahdi to carry a weapon. Should he use it to kill an unarmed civilian, it would most definitely spell disaster for the Major.

The team raided the factory and rounded up five men who identified themselves as employees. All willingly presented the Major with IDs and Fahdi verified their employment by matching the names to those found on a work schedule and other paperwork in the factory office. Major Warren had Fahdi scan all documents for anything suspicious. He thumbed through a stack and reported to the Major that everything looked legitimate.

"It was just a stack of your average business paperwork—schedules, accounting reports, contracts, and the like—nothing important or dubious. No affidavits declaring 'so-and-so is a terrorist' or any maps leading to Al-Zarqawi's hide out or anything," Fahdi jested.

The team cleared every room in the building, opened every door, searched every closet, and peeked in every nook and cranny. The only people in the factory were the workers and the only weapon found was an AK-47 that, upon inspection, had not been fired anytime recently.

Although the men were legitimate employees of the factory, it did not necessarily mean they had nothing to do with the IED. But the Major had nothing to prove otherwise, and, therefore, had to release them. In all likelihood, one of the guys had probably been outside smoking a cigarette or watching the convoy pass, then ducked inside for cover after the explosion occurred.

Again, they'd been attacked by a ghost.

The team returned to the convoy as the medivac choppers landed to pick up the dead and wounded. Since two of the Humvees were completely disabled, they waited on the road until tow trucks from TQ arrived to haul the vehicles back to Camp Manhattan.

After dark, Major Warren gathered his Marines and told them he wanted to return to the site of the IED attack and pay a visit to any homes within a mile radius, hoping that if any of the locals did know or see something, they'd be more willing to talk to the Americans under the cover of night. As this was an impromptu mission that fell outside of the Civil Affairs team's official capacity, Major Warren informed the men that accompanying him on the assignment was completely voluntary.

Everyone, including Fahdi, grabbed their gear.

The team drove out to the IED site and spent several hours patrolling the area on foot, paying visits to all the homes in the area. The locals were all aware of the day's event. But as usual, no one had any information regarding who was behind the attack and the team returned to base emptyhanded.

The next day, the team traveled to another village outside Fallujah. A little larger than the previous village they'd worked in, it was built around a large government-owned Sulphur plant that had been the main employer of the village residents. Of course, the plant had been shut down since the war and Major Warren wanted to see what he could do to get it back up and running, and hopefully put the people in the village back to work. The village also had a small police station that a U.S. Army reconstruction unit had paid local contractors to rebuild several months prior. The station was subsequently bombed to the ground so the Army had it rebuilt again, and again, it was bombed. The Army had given up after the second go-round and told Major Warren "good luck" upon his decision to have it rebuilt a third time. The Major didn't want to arbitrarily rebuild the station but wanted to get to the bottom of why this particular police station was being constantly targeted. There were several other village police stations in the area that hadn't even had a rock thrown at them. What was so special about this one that made insurgents want to keep it in ruins?

Another aspect intrigued the Major: none of the police were ever harmed in any of the bombings. They were always warned of an impending attack and allowed to escape before the insurgents showed up. Major Warren questioned the police unit's commander as to why he and his men never made a stand to defend the station. The police commander told the Major that since they are a small satellite station, there are only eight officers assigned to the location and the insurgents who show up to raid and bomb the building are always a group of at least fifteen to twenty men. "It would be suicide for us to try and fight back," the commander declared.

"Are you telling me you just step outside and toss them the keys when they show up, allowing them to make off with all your weapons and gear before leveling the place to the ground?" Major Warren pressed, dumbfounded.

"Well, the U.S. military guys before you, who rebuilt the station, gave us the phone number of a local Army unit to call when the insurgents show up or threaten to attack, but by the time you guys get here, the assholes are long gone," the commander defended.

"Do you have any idea why they are so hell-bent on bombing this station?" Major Warren asked, then waited for Fahdi to translate. "There are other satellite stations exactly like this one in neighboring villages that haven't had any issues. What is so special about this station?"

"We believe we are being targeted because the road the station is on is used as a supply line for Al-Qaeda traveling north and south," the commander rationalized. "It's a convenient yet desolate route to use to get in and out of Baghdad. It's a straight shot but runs through the middle of nowhere."

The police commander's theory was weak but possible, and Major Warren vowed to rebuild the station and fortify it with extra men and defenses to withstand a future attack.

The next day, the Civil Affairs team returned to the police station to meet with the commander and the local Iraqi construction contractor who had organized the rebuilding of the police station twice before. Since he had done it before,

Major Warren decided to hire him to rebuild the station a third time, with a few upgrades and design modifications.

The contractor laid out the blueprints, walked the Major through the timeline for construction and then informed him how much everything was going to cost. When the contractor declared the total cost for the station would be $400,000, Fahdi's eyes practically bulged from his skull and he guffawed, thinking the contractor was joking.

"What's wrong?" Major Warren asked. Since the contractor had said the number in Arabic, he had no clue what had triggered Fahdi's reaction.

"He says the total cost for the station is going to be $400,000," Fahdi told the Major.

"Okay," Major Warren responded nonchalantly. "Okay? What do you mean, okay? You could build a fucking castle in this area for that amount of money," Fahdi answered, not sure now if he was more shocked by the $400,000 price tag or Major Warren's flippancy toward it. "It's a ridiculous amount! They are scamming you."

"Well, tell him to break down all the costs to justify the $400,000," Major Warren told Fahdi.

Fahdi translated Major Warren's request and the contractor told Fahdi how he calculated the $400,000 price tag.

"First of all, you've got to factor in that we've got to pay the workers more money than the usual salary around here because they are risking their lives working on a U.S. sanctioned project," the contractor reasoned. "And getting all the material here from Baghdad is extremely expensive. There are very few people left who are willing to drive a truck here. Drivers are being killed or kidnapped left and right. Finally, 40% of that $400,000 will have to be paid to Al-Qaeda and resistance groups who now control large stretches of road between here and Baghdad. If you want the supplies to come through, the driver will have to pay to get through the insurgent checkpoints. Last time we built the police station, 30% of the total price went to paying off the groups. I'm confident now that amount will be closer to 40%, so I have to factor it in."

"Hey, at least the dude was honest, but the Major damn near shit his pants hearing what the contractor said about paying off Al-Qaeda."

"What? You're taking U.S. money intended to build a police station and giving it to Al-Qaeda?" Major Warren shrieked in anger.

The contractor shrugged his shoulders. "Unless you're willing to escort all the supplies here yourself, there's no way around it. And even if you do escort it, I don't think I could convince any of my guys to drive a truck in the middle of an American convoy. If he isn't killed in an attack meant for you during the drive, he'll surely be skinned alive later on when people find out he's driving trucks across the country for the Americans."

"How about this," Major Warren replied. "What if we handle every aspect of transporting the materials here from Baghdad, using *our* trucks and *our* drivers?"

"Well, in that case, I can get the station built for $200,000."

"Perfect. Then we're in agreement," Major Warren declared. "Let's get it done."

Over the next two weeks, the Civil Affairs team supervised the rebuilding of the police station, ensuring everything was carried out according to the Major's instructions and standards. He had them erect watchtowers at all four corners and installed heavy machine guns in each tower. Major Warren also increased the number of officers assigned to the station to twenty and equipped the armory with additional weapons and SWAT gear.

With the rebuild and rearmament of the police station complete, Major Warren met with the commander. "Now that I've provided all of this for you, I'm going to need you to do something in return," Major Warren told the commander. "I do not want to hear about this place being overrun ever again. You need to promise to do everything in your power to hold this place against any future attacks. Do you understand?"

The commander nodded.

"In other words," Major Warren continued, "the next time this station gets bombed, your ass better be inside it." But the Major rethought his last statement and grabbed Fahdi's arm to stop him before he translated it to the commander. "Don't translate that. Just tell him I need him to promise to do his best to defend the station and keep it secure."

"I wish I'd have gone ahead and translated the Major's original statement," Fahdi said regrettably. "I had a feeling that police commander was a slimy, conniving bastard the first time we talked to him. We later found out the entire circus with the police station being repeatedly bombed was an inside job. The commander himself, several of his officers, and a few of the villagers were behind the whole thing. The Americans would pay to build and equip the station, the commander would hire some "insurgents" to come in and raid the place for all the weapons and gear, and then blow the building up. Afterwards they'd sell everything on the black market and pocket the cash. They were even getting a kick-back from the local construction company the Americans kept hiring to rebuild the place. They had themselves a sweet little racket going on. Too bad we didn't put the pieces together before that asshole commander tried to take us down."

After hearing various bits of information through the grapevine regarding the commander's involvement in the bombings of his own station, Major Warren grew suspicious and the Civil Affairs team spent a few days conducting their own investigation into the matter. They spoke to locals, interviewed employees from the construction company hired to rebuild the station, and questioned the commander's own men individually to see if there were any inconsistencies in their stories.

Having gathered sufficient evidence against the commander, the Major decided to confront him. The Civil Affairs team paid a visit to the police station and Major Warren launched an impromptu interrogation on the commander.

Two hours into questioning the commander, Sergeant Ramirez and Sergeant Santos, who were standing watch outside the police station while the Major, Fahdi, and Sergeant Vallejo were inside with the commander, burst into the station screaming their convoy, parked a half-mile down the road from the station, was taking fire. The Civil Affairs team took off at a sprint toward the convoy as a full-fledged firefight erupted between the convoy soldiers and an unknown number of insurgents spraying AK fire onto the vehicles from a cloaked position within a patch of palm trees a couple hundred yards south of the road.

By the time the team reached the convoy, the U.S. soldiers had advanced into the trees and pushed the enemy into a defensive retreat. The Americans cornered their attackers in a small farm house and promptly surrounded the residence. A small team was assembled to go in and clear the house, but as usual, all they found inside were two freshly discharged AK-47 rifles and several of the black and red checkered scarves the insurgents typically wore to cover their faces strewn across the floor.

Everyone was flabbergasted. How did they manage to escape? Again, they'd vanished into thin air.

"No one had a clue how these guys got away. It was like going after phantoms; they were there one minute and gone the next. It was fucking unbelievable."

When the members of the convoy regrouped, a few, including Major Warren and a couple of his Marines, returned to investigate the area the insurgents had launched their attack from. A brief analysis of all the evidence led Major Warren to believe the incident was too organized to be a random attack; that someone had tipped the insurgents off regarding the convoy's location and he had a good idea who had done the "tipping."

The Civil Affairs team hiked back to the police station to resume their questioning of the police commander. Although Warren was nearly positive either the commander himself or members of his squad were behind the attack on the convoy, and knew he had no concrete evidence to prove his theory, he decided to lay out some bait. After feigning an apology for putting the commander through the wringer earlier in the day, Major Warren instructed Fahdi to tell the commander the team would return to the station the next day at 11 a.m. to discuss ordering more equipment and supplies for the station to replace those that had been stolen during the last break-in.

This took Fahdi by surprise and he shot the Major a confused look before translating what he'd said. The Major had not told anyone, aside from his own Marines, exactly when and where the team would be operating. Fahdi typically never even knew where they were going until they got there. He was afraid the Major had made an unintentional gaffe, but Warren was persistent.

"Tell him we will be here at precisely 11 a.m. tomorrow," Major Warren reiterated in a firm tone loud enough for all within earshot to hear. Fahdi was not catching on to what the Major was trying to do, but did as ordered.

On the way back to the base, Fahdi couldn't hold back any longer and decided to question the Major's decision to tell the shady commander such privileged tactical information. "Major, considering this is such a hot area," Fahdi began in a diplomatic tone, "do you think it was a good idea to tell everyone back there when and where we'd be? Or were you just feeding them bullshit?"

"Nope, not bullshit," the Major replied nonchalantly. "I have every intention of being at that police station at 11 a.m. tomorrow morning."

Fahdi sat for several long seconds in silent confusion.

"We're picking a fight, Allen," Warren finally admitted. "I know that commander is a fucking, backstabbing shithead, but I've got nothing solid to prove it. We want them to be waiting for us tomorrow, thinking they're going to get the jump on us. It will A) provide proof that those assholes are collaborating with the insurgency, and B) give us a chance to flush them out in a legitimate open battle."

"So, we intentionally set ourselves up to walk right into a raging shit storm tomorrow?"

Major Warren smiled. "Exactly."

"You know, I just remembered, I've got plans tomorrow. I don't think I'm going to be able to make it to work."

"Whatever, Allen. Don't be a pussy," Major Warren jested. "After all, this is your fucking country."

"It is, but you guys are fucking crazy!"

CHAPTER ELEVEN

YOU GUYS ARE FUCKING CRAZY

JUNE 2004

The Civil Affairs team awoke the next morning and prepared themselves for a fight. Luckily, they were going to have extra backup. In addition to the regular Army unit who typically accompanied them on their daily patrols, they would also be joined by a Marine squad of about a dozen troops as well as an eighteen-man Army QRF (Quick Reaction Forces) unit. Major Warren had met with the QRF's Officer in Charge, Captain Gellar, the night before and explained the situation he'd "arranged" to ensure everyone was properly informed and ready for whatever may happen. He told Gellar the convoy would probably be rolling right into an organized ambush.

As the convoy formed up near the gate of the base, Fahdi stood leaning up against the rear fender of Major Warren's Humvee anticipating the order to mount up and roll out. While waiting, he noticed some sideways glances from a few of the

QRF soldiers as they walked by and overheard a few whispers regarding his being armed with an AK-47.

Shit.

Several minutes later, the Major approached him with a solemn expression. Fahdi already knew what he was going to say.

"Look, Allen, I'm really sorry to have to do this, but I'm going to need you to leave your AK behind today. The QRF commander isn't comfortable with you being armed while riding in their convoy."

"Seriously?" Fahdi replied dejectedly. "We're about to walk into a shit storm. What am I supposed to do, throw sand in the insurgents' eyes when they shoot at me?"

Major Warren dodged the question. "Go run your rifle over to the Civil Affairs tent and secure it in my footlocker," Major Warren said, handing Fahdi a set of keys.

"This is such bullshit," Fahdi muttered under his breath as he headed for tent. He'd expected the Major to stick up for him at least a little, but it appeared Major Warren hadn't uttered a word in Fahdi's defense. He considered returning to the convoy and telling the Major he refused to attend the mission if they denied him the ability to carry a weapon, but reconsidered. Working for the Civil Affairs team was a challenge, but it had benefits, and he honestly enjoyed his position as their translator. If he refused a mission, he'd shatter all credibility and ruin any relationship he'd worked so hard to build with the team. It wasn't worth it.

Fahdi returned to the Humvee with his teeth clenched and refused to make eye contact with anyone in the convoy, including the Civil Affairs Marines, but kept his mouth shut. He opened the back door of the Humvee to take his usual spot in the middle of the backseat and was grabbed from the back by his body armor and pulled out of the vehicle. He spun around to see who had ahold of him and came nose to nose with Sergeant Vallejo, whose expression Fahdi was unable discern.

"Put your arms up! We need to make sure you got your vest on properly," Vallejo barked loudly in an unusually firm tone. He then gave Fahdi a little shove backwards and Fahdi stumbled into someone else behind him. Fahdi turned his head and saw he'd been pushed into Major Warren. Before Fahdi could get a word out, Vallejo said again, "Arms up, man." Fahdi reluctantly lifted his arms and Vallejo began patting and running his hands up, down, and around Fahdi's body armor. At the same time, Fahdi felt the Major quickly lift the back of his uniform top and slip something into the waistband of his pants. Fahdi immediately knew what it was—a .9mm. "Looks good," Vallejo announced completing the ruse. "Hop in."

Fahdi wondered why they'd gone through such a big show to slip him a pistol when they could have given it to him in the Humvee where no one would have noticed. A few seconds later, he realized why. An Army QRF sergeant hopped into the driver's seat of the Humvee. One of the QRF commander's requests from the night before was that a member of his team was to drive each of the vehicles in the convoy.

A few minutes before 11 a.m., the convoy pulled up and parked in the exact same position they'd been when they were attacked the previous day. Everyone was on ultra-high alert, but the area was quiet.

"Let's head for the police station," Major Warren finally said after they sat there for nearly twenty minutes without incident. The Civil Affairs team, along with the extra Marine unit, dismounted from the vehicles and began hiking the half mile to the police station while the QRF team and the other Army soldiers remained with the convoy.

With everything appearing normal at the police station as well, he decided the team may as well get something done while they waited to be attacked.

The Civil Affairs team entered the police station to resume discussions about supplies and equipment while the extra Marines formed a perimeter around the station. The team spent the next couple of hours buttoning up their rearmament plans with the police station and going about their usual duties. In the early afternoon, convinced the insurgents weren't taking the bait and his trap wasn't going to work, Major Warren told the extra Marine unit they may as well return to base.

The team finished their work at the police station in mid-afternoon and began the walk back to the convoy. About 100 yards from the convoy, all hell broke loose.

"Take cover!" Major Warren screamed as echoes of AK-47 and small arms fire rang out from across the field to the team's right. Bullets rained down on their position and Fahdi could hear rounds pinging off the vehicles of the convoy parked along the dirt road.

"We started getting fired on, like seriously fired on. We were taking rounds from AKs, RPKs, PKCs, mortars, you name it, they were shooting it at us. Since we were too far to make a run for the convoy vehicles, we ran a couple dozen yards off the side of the road and dropped down in the field. The attack was being launched from a cluster of houses sitting on the far side of the field we'd darted into, putting us between the insurgents and our convoy.

"Considering how intense the attack was, and the fact we'd sent home half of our back-up, I figured we'd try to get to the convoy and hightail it out of there; perhaps come back later with more help and clean out the area. But Major Warren never left nor ran from a fight. He'd stay until either we were all dead, the people firing at us were all dead, or the shooting stopped. The QRF team must have seen where we ended up because they turned several of the convoy vehicles off the road and started coming through the field toward us. I guess to pick us up or at least provide some cover fire for us."

As soon as the Humvees reached the Civil Affairs team's position, Major Warren turned to Fahdi and shouted, "Allen! Get your ass in one of the Humvees!" Fahdi low-crawled to the nearest Humvee and scrambled into the back seat. Without a rifle, he wasn't much use and knew it was better to stay out of the way for the time being.

Major Warren and the rest of the Civil Affairs team pushed on toward the houses the insurgents were firing from while the Humvees crept along behind them laying down cover fire. Fahdi continued to hear the tick-tick-tick of rounds bouncing off his vehicle. A few minutes later, there was a lull in the gunfire. Fahdi poked his head up and peered out the window of the Humvee. He saw Major Warren and the team now running towards the houses on the far end of the field.

Within minutes, the enemy fire resumed. They had merely halted to reload and/or relocate to better firing positions. A few seconds after, there was a massive BOOM! and Fahdi saw one of the Humvees in the convoy nearly roll on its side and burst into flames. Two insurgents had managed to flank the convoy and get a clear shot off from an RPG into the front right fender of one of the vehicles.

Fahdi, inside one of the Humvees, realized the vehicles were sitting ducks that simply made great targets for the enemy. He slipped out the back door and started crawling through the field trying to catch up with Major Warren and the rest of the team. Merely twenty yards into his crawl, the Humvee he'd just exited was the second one hit with an RPG.

Fahdi finally caught up to Sergeant Juarez, who was covering the rear of the group. "The Major told you to stay in the Humvee!" Juarez shouted at Fahdi.

"They're blowing them up!" Fahdi retorted. "I rather be on foot with you guys."

The enemy fire trailed off again and the Marines popped up to get their bearings and regroup. Noticing they were an uncomfortable distance behind the rest of the group, Sergeant Juarez and Fahdi jumped to their feet and made a mad dash to catch up. Only a few yards into their sprint the distinct pop, pop of AK fire started again, resuming more quickly this time than before. The enemy had either gotten faster at reloading or had only stopped in hopes the Marines would reveal their positions. Sergeant Juarez and Fahdi both dropped to the ground again, but it was too late. Before Fahdi's knees hit the grass, a searing pain struck his chest and knocked him back several feet. Sprawled out flat on his back staring up at the clear blue sky, he felt like he'd been hit by a truck. The air was sucked out of his lungs and he gasped to catch his breath. Sergeant Juarez threw his body protectively over Fahdi's in an attempt to shield him from further wounds. But as Juarez's weight fell on top of him it made it even more difficult for Fahdi to get the air he desperately needed back into his lungs.

Once Fahdi finally caught his breath, he noticed the blood. "I've been shot!" he screamed. "Get off me!" Fahdi struggled to push the massive Marine Sergeant off. Considering the extensive amount of pain and blood, Fahdi was sure the bullet had pierced through his body armor.

"Stay the fuck down!" Sergeant Juarez yelled back.

"I'm hit! It went through!" Fahdi continued to yell and squirm under Juarez's weight. He was having severe difficulty breathing and feared the bullet had struck a lung. Seconds later, two U.S.

combat choppers appeared overhead to provide air support. They showered the houses with suppressive fire until the enemy shooting ceased for good. Sergeant Juarez sat up and straddled Fahdi, holding him down to survey the damage.

"Where are you hit?" Juarez screamed.

"My chest!" Fahdi blurted. Blood was smeared all over the front of Fahdi's uniform and across his body armor. "Oh fuck! Oh fuck! I'm bleeding bad!" He was in a lot of pain but also relieved because he knew the pain meant he probably wasn't dying.

Sergeant Juarez ripped the Velcro straps from Fahdi's bullet proof vest and pushed the armor up over his head. He ran his hands up and down Fahdi's chest and stomach and across his shoulders.

"There's nothing Allen! It didn't go through. You're fine."

"But I'm bleeding!" Fahdi argued.

"No, you're not," Juarez replied in a surprisingly calm tone. "I am."

Fahdi saw Sergeant Juarez's uniform, near the top corner of his right shoulder, was ripped. Blood was seeping from the area and dripping down his arm. He'd been grazed by a round, perhaps the same one that took Fahdi down. Juarez had thrown his body over Fahdi's and bled onto him, covering Fahdi in in more blood than himself.

"Shit, dude, you're hit!" Fahdi said, now shifting his focus from his own injuries to Sergeant Juarez's shoulder wound. "We've gotta' get you to a medic."

"It's fine. It looks worse than it really is. I only got grazed," Juarez said as he grabbed Fahdi's vest and looked at it. His finger found the indentation where the AK round that took Fahdi down was embedded deep into one of the vest's chest plates. "See," he said pointing it out to Fahdi, "the bullet that got you is right here. Put your vest back on, we've got to catch back up with the Major."

Fahdi pulled the body armor vest back over his head and strapped it on. He glanced down and noticed the bullet was lodged in the area right over his heart. *Holy fuck! I'd have been dead.*

Before the two continued on, Fahdi told Juarez to let him have a look at his shoulder. Fahdi pulled apart the material of Juarez's uniform where it'd been ripped and analyzed the wound. It was a superficial gash and the bleeding had already stopped.

"Alright, man, I guess you're ok," Fahdi said wiping the blood off his fingers onto his pants.

The two got to their feet and managed to catch up with the rest of the team. Fahdi's shoulder and chest areas were throbbing, but he pushed through the pain, simply happy to be alive.

The team made it to the houses the insurgents had been firing from, but as usual, all they found were spent shells of every shape and size: AK, PKC, etc. No actual weapons had been left behind and, of course, not a soul in site.

An hour later, Major Warren decided to call off the hunt and head back to base. In addition to Juarez and Fahdi, a couple other guys in the convoy had been injured. One of the soldiers in the first Humvee hit by an RPG sustained some burns and a few others bore some minor injuries, but thankfully, no one had been seriously injured or killed.

"By the time we were halfway back to the base, I was in so much pain I was almost crying. It probably would have been less painful to take a clean hit in the arm or leg than a direct hit to the chest with the body armor on. The armor spreads out the concussion of the bullet, making it feel like you've been hit by a car. I couldn't move my arms and it hurt to breathe, but I didn't want to bitch and complain because I knew the Major was pissed about how his plan had blown up in his face."

Although he was seething over the day's incident, Major Warren sympathized with Fahdi, seeing clearly the agony etched all over his face. "Allen, are you okay?"

"My shoulder hurts like a mother fucker," Fahdi replied between noticeably labored breaths. "I'm just . . . in pain."

Major Warren hopped on the radio, ordered the entire convoy to halt and for Sergeant Goldberg, the team medic, to come to their vehicle to have a look at Fahdi.

Sergeant Goldberg took one look at Fahdi and pulled out a morphine injection. "This should relax you," Goldberg said as he stuck Fahdi in the leg. "Are you having trouble breathing?" he asked after administering the pain killer.

"Well, I know it hurts *when* I breathe," Fahdi replied.

"He could have some broken ribs, perhaps even a collapsed lung from the impact of the bullet," Goldberg reported to the Major. "I need to remove his body armor to know for sure."

"No, we are too exposed here. We're only about fifteen minutes from TQ. They have a full field hospital there, Allen, I'd rather they checked you out."

The convoy rolled into TQ and Sergeant Goldberg escorted Fahdi to the hospital. Goldberg relayed Fahdi's status to the intake nurse and within minutes one of the doctors, an Army Colonel, showed up to examine Fahdi's injuries. He immediately saw the round in Fahdi's body armor and announced with a smile, "Congratulations! You're officially a Marine today!"

"Super," Fahdi replied sarcastically, "but it hurts like a mother fucker."

"And you already talk like one, too," the Colonel added smiling. "That's bonus points! Now let's get that vest off and see what the damage is."

Easier said than done. Fahdi was in such intense pain there

was no way he could even raise his arms up enough to get the vest off over his head; technically the only way to get it off.

"No problem, we'll just cut it off," the doctor suggested.

At that, Fahdi panicked. "No! The Major will kill me if I cut up his extra vest!"

"I'm fairly certain he'll understand," the doctor replied.

"No, he probably will be pissed," Goldberg interjected. "Here, I'll take out all the plates to lighten it up and make it a little more flexible. See if that works."

Armored plates removed, Fahdi, with the help of both the doctor and Goldberg, wriggled out of the vest without damaging it. The Colonel sent Fahdi for some chest x-rays while Goldberg went to work on digging the bullet out of Fahdi's vest.

The doctor examined Fahdi's x-rays and relayed the good news: no broken ribs, no collapsed lungs, no internal bleeding. "You're going to have some serious bruising and be in a bit of pain over the next few days, but other than that you're going to be just fine. I'll give you some anti-inflammatories to get you through. I know it doesn't seem like it right now, but you were very lucky."

Goldberg handed Fahdi what was left of the bullet he'd been hit with. "Here's a memento, buddy." It looked like nothing more than a thick penny but still identifiable—an AK-47 round.

CHAPTER TWELVE

PAYBACK'S A BITCH

JULY 2004

Major Warren gave Fahdi a few days off to recover from his injuries. The morning after his close call, Fahdi removed his shirt to take a shower and surveyed the damage in the mirror. The entire front of his body was a grotesquely unnatural black color from his neck clear down to his waistline and around both sides of his ribcage.

On the second day of Fahdi's convalescence, Major Warren stopped by to check up on him. Fahdi lifted his shirt to show off his "battle scars" and the Major simply reiterated how lucky Fahdi was to come through with nothing more than a gnarly bruise. Before leaving, he tossed Fahdi his satellite phone, telling him he'd earned the right to call his family.

"I got ahold of my mom, which really eased my mind. I hadn't talked to anyone in my family in nearly two months and I was really worried about them. She told me some of the neighbors had been snooping around and asking questions regarding my whereabouts; said some people had relayed they thought they'd seen me around Ramadi. Not good. She and my brother were telling everyone I was up in Mosul working with my Uncles, but it was becoming hard to keep up the ruse. Even though it was extremely risky, I knew I needed to make an appearance back home to corroborate my mom's story, for my family's sake. I also missed them. It was the longest stretch I'd ever been away from my family."

Taking the satellite phone, Warren immediately knew by the look on Fahdi's face something was up.

"What's wrong? You look upset. Is everything okay back home?"

"I'm going to need to head home for a couple of days," Fahdi replied.

"Of course," the Major said nodding his head, then added in a solemn tone. "Will you be coming back?"

"Yes, I'll come back. I promise. All I need is two days."

Fahdi returned to his trailer and cleaned out his wallet, careful to remove all identifying papers and paraphernalia that could be used to link him to the Americans: PX receipts, ID cards, badges, phone numbers of any U.S. sat phones or base offices, etc. He dressed in his civilian clothes and, on his way to the main gate, stopped by the Civil Affairs tent to give Major Warren his Titan badge and base ID. It was a relief to find the Major alone. The guys were all on a run. Fahdi was glad he could avoid explaining his leaving. They'd all think he was quitting and running away because of his injury.

At 3 p.m., he blended in with a group of local Iraqi workers on the cleaning crew and exited the base as they did. Considering the danger Fahdi and other translators faced working for the Americans and being caught outside the bases, he wondered how workers on the cleaning crews typically came and went and lived in the local communities without being harassed. He later learned many of them were on Al-Qaeda's payroll and were providing them with any useful info they managed to pick up while working inside the base.

"Outside the base, I got about 200 yards down the street and it hit me how bad an idea it really was."

To get to Baghdad, Fahdi would to have to go through Fallujah. Given the vast number of citizens inside Fallujah who'd seen him working with the Civil Affairs team, it was almost certain he'd run into someone who recognized him—not good. His only other option in order to bypass Fallujah was to backtrack to Ramadi and either take a roundabout way north or south, then circle back to Baghdad, but his face would be just as recognizable in Ramadi as in Fallujah. He also knew, even if he did manage to make it to Baghdad, he *wouldn't* be able to make it back on his own and *would* be stuck between a rock and a hard place. He did an about face and hightailed it back to the base.

Fahdi approached the gate of the camp and was handled in the typical way they dealt with locals trying to gain access to the base. The soldiers on duty didn't recognize him, he had no identification on him, and the Major didn't expect him back for two days. Getting back onto the base was going to be a feat in itself.

About 100 feet from the gate, the MP ordered him to "*Stop!*" through a loud speaker from the gatehouse. Fahdi knew the drill. He stopped in his tracks and ensured his hands were visible.

"Pull up your shirt!" The soldier demanded. Step one in screening locals approaching the base: make sure they don't have an explosive vest strapped to their chest.

Fahdi complied and lifted his shirt up to his neck, hoping the nasty discoloration from his injury wouldn't cause any issues.

"Turn around!" the soldier ordered. Again, Fahdi did as he was told. "Okay, you may approach—slowly!"

Fahdi practically tiptoed up to the guard shack. One of the soldiers stepped out with his M-16 leveled at Fahdi's chest. "What the hell is wrong with your chest?" the soldier barked.

"It's a long story."

"Whatever. Who are you and what do you want?" the soldier asked gruffly.

Fahdi explained he was a Titan translator and worked for Major Warren's Civil Affairs Unit.

"Where is your badge?" the soldier asked suspiciously.

"It's inside the base."

"Why is it inside the base? Not very smart to leave it in there while you're out here?"

Fahdi wanted to say, 'Actually, it is, considering if I were caught with it out here I'd be dead.' But he wasn't about to be condescending to a teenage American aiming an automatic rifle at him. "Can you radio Major Warren with the Civil Affairs team and tell him I'm here. He'll vouch for me. I even have his satellite phone number if you want to call him."

The soldier stepped back inside the guard house and radioed the Civil Affairs team. Relief flooded Fahdi as Sergeant Santos' voice answered back over the radio.

"May I please speak with Major Warren?" the soldier asked Santos.

"The Major is currently at chow," Santos replied. "Is it urgent?"

"Well, there's a local here at the main gate. Says his name is 'Allen' and that he's your team's translator. He's trying to regain entry to the base but doesn't have his badges. He told me they're with Major Warren."

After a pause, Sergeant Santos finally answered, "As far as I know, our linguist is here on the base."

Fahdi's heart fell into his stomach. *Shit, the Major still hasn't told the guys I left.*

"Roger that," the soldier replied and dropped the radio. "Well, you're obviously not the Civil Affairs' Team's translator because they said their translator is with them."

"Trust me, I am their translator. The guys on the team simply don't know yet that I was leaving for a few days to go home. I literally exited the base a few minutes ago with the workers. Please call the team again and ask to talk to Major Warren. He knows what is going on."

"I'm not calling him away from his chow," the soldier replied. "But if you want to come back in an hour, I'll radio the unit again and see if he's available. In the meantime, you can't hang out around here. You'll need to head back at least as far as the main road."

Fahdi did as instructed and walked back to the highway. He sat down off the side of the road and did his best to keep his head down and appear inconspicuous, praying no one driving by would recognize him. With no shade anywhere nearby, Fahdi endured the direct intensity of the merciless July sun while he sat and stared at his watch, counting the minutes as they slowly ticked by.

"It was the longest hour of my life. Looking back on it, I guess it really wasn't that big of a deal. But at the time, I was scared to death, more scared than I'd ever been. I was sure a truck full of Al-Qaeda was going to drive by and grab me."

After exactly one hour had passed, Fahdi returned to the base entrance and submitted to the same security procedure: lift your shirt, turn around, etc. Cleared to approach the gate, Fahdi went up to the soldier who'd sent him away earlier, "Well, I guess you know why I'm here."

The soldier nodded, grabbed his radio, and called up the Civil

Affairs HQ. Fahdi practically cried tears of joy as the Major's voice came through the receiver.

Thank God!

Major Warren confirmed Fahdi's identity and said he'd send one of his men up to the gate with Fahdi's IDs.

A few minutes later, Sergeant Goldberg showed up and presented Fahdi's Titan employee and base access badges to the gate guards who then happily cleared Fahdi to enter the camp.

"You want me to take you to see the Major or do you just want to go to your room," Goldberg asked Fahdi as they climbed into the Humvee.

"Take me to my room. I need a shower. I've been sweating my balls off out there."

"Out where?" Goldberg asked confused.

"Outside the base, sitting on the side of the road, waiting for the Major to get done eating so he could verify who I was to the gate guards."

"Oh shit, man! How long were you waiting?"

"I've been stuck out there for the past hour. They radioed Santos, but he didn't know I'd gone home. He told them I was on the base. They thought I was lying about who I was and sent me away."

"That doesn't make any sense, Major Warren told us all this morning you were going home to Baghdad for a few days. I was wondering why you were back so soon."

"Wait, you guys knew I was leaving since this morning? Then why the fuck did Santos tell the gate guard I was on base? He acted like he had no idea I'd left to go home."

"I don't know. Maybe he wasn't paying attention when the Major told us about you leaving."

"He almost got my ass killed! Change of plans. Take me to Major Warren," Fahdi demanded angrily.

"Look, I understand how you feel right now," Goldberg said in an attempt to calm Fahdi down, "but it's not a good idea to be a rat. You don't want these guys to have any reason not to cover your ass out on a mission. Santos probably didn't realize you'd left already. You know, I'm not even sure now if he was around when the Major told us."

"If it was an honest mistake, then that's fine. But I want to find out!"

Arriving at the Civil Affairs tent, Fahdi marched inside and told Major Warren of his ordeal. The Major ordered Goldberg to find Santos and bring him to the tent, then confronted Santos who played it off as if he had no idea Fahdi had already left the base.

"Fine, even if you thought I was on base, who the hell do you think would be calling you guys from the gate and saying they are your translator? The gate guard even told you my name was 'Allen!' Who else would be standing up there saying their name is Allen and they work for you?" Fahdi pressed.

"Look, man, I honestly didn't know you had left yet."

"Fine, whatever," Fahdi finally said, feeling Santos was hiding something.

Major Warren dismissed Santos, then turned to Fahdi. "Why didn't you go home?"

"I really wanted to," Fahdi said dejectedly, "but I didn't think I'd make it. It dawned on me that half the Iraqi National Guard guys running the checkpoints between here and Baghdad might be ones I helped train back in Ramadi. I could have easily run into one who'd recognize me and probably sell me out to Al-Qaeda.

"I think you made a good call not to go," the Major agreed. "I wish I could help you out, but there's really nothing I can do."

"I understand, sir," Fahdi said and went to his room.

* * *

The next morning, as Fahdi was eating breakfast with the team, Santos came over and sat down across from him. "So, what did they do to you yesterday at the gate?" Santos asked.

Fahdi gave him a quick rundown of his hour in hell. "Payback's a bitch isn't it," Santos said with a smirk.

Fahdi dropped his fork and shot Santos and angry look. "Excuse me?"

"Remember that day you and Sergeant Goldberg were sitting around making fun of me for about an hour. I told you I'd get you back."

"Are you fucking serious? This was your idea of a goddamn prank? You could have gotten me killed, asshole!"

"I had no idea they'd make you sit alone by the highway. I thought they'd just hold you there at the gate house. I swear."

"They treated me like a damn terrorist!" Fahdi screamed. He stood up from the table and stormed out of the chow hall, headed for Major Warren, but Sergeant Goldberg ran after him.

"I'm not going to tell you not to tell the Major," Goldberg said as he fell in step with Fahdi's determined march toward the Civil Affairs tent. "You have every right to be pissed. But again, what good is it going to do? It's only going to cause a rift that, in the long run, is going to hurt you more than anyone. Santos honestly considered it a harmless prank. He had no idea it put your life at risk. I would understand, and some of the other guys may understand, why you're telling the Major, but most of them are simply going to think of you as a rat. And trust me, you don't want that."

Fahdi halted and turned to face Goldberg. "You can honestly look me in the eye right now and tell me he truly didn't understand the kind of risk he put me in yesterday?"

"Allen, I swear, he really feels awful about it. He didn't know."

Fahdi changed direction and went to his room. He had a couple of days off to recover from his injury, most of which were locked in his trailer, avoiding any interaction with the Civil Affairs Marines. He needed some space and time to vent.

"I was beyond pissed and I felt betrayed. But over the next couple of days I calmed down. I knew those guys simply didn't comprehend how dangerous it was for me to be outside on my own. And, after all, I was the one responsible for putting myself in that situation to begin with. They assumed, since I was a local Iraqi, I could just blend in and be fine. They had no idea posters of me were hanging up in mosques in Ramadi and it wasn't common knowledge amongst the Americans yet that the insurgency was offering money to people who captured or killed translators working for the Americans."

Fahdi decided to have a little heart to heart with the Civil Affairs team after he'd given himself time to cool down and think about what should be said. He made it abundantly clear what kind of danger translators like him faced outside the protective walls of U.S. camps and bases. Several months later, the *Associated Press* published a story on the extreme risks and dangers translators who worked for the U.S. military in Iraq faced on a daily basis. Below is an excerpt from the article:

> *It's one of the most dangerous civilian jobs in one of the world's most dangerous countries: translating Arabic for the U.S. military in Iraq.*
>
> *One by one, little noticed in the daily mayhem, dozens of inter- preters have been killed. They account for 40% of the 300-plus death claims filed by private contractors with the U.S. Labor Department. Riding in bomb-blasted Humvees, tagging along on foot patrols in Fallujah or dashing into buildings behind Marines, translators are*

dying on the job, but also facing danger at home; hunted by insur-
gents who call them pro-American collaborators.

The efficiency with which insurgents hunt down Titan contrac-
tors worried the U.S. military. As militants killed them in growing
numbers, usually in ambushes off base, the Army and others began
housing Titan workers on military bases or in Baghdad's fortified
Green Zone.

"There was a period when it seemed translators were being targeted
on a daily basis," said First Sgt. Stephen Valley, a U.S. Army reservist
who worked with Arab journalists in Baghdad. "There is virtually no
way to protect these people." (Krane, 2005)

The Civil Affairs team convoy was headed out on a mission a
week after the incident and drove past a local guy sitting alone
on the side of the road in almost the exact same place Fahdi had
been sitting a few days earlier. "Gee, that looks familiar," Fahdi
commented sarcastically.

"Oh, yeah," Major Warren replied. "Sorry again about all that."

Fahdi tried to bite his tongue, but could no longer keep it in.
"Oh, by the way, Sergeant Santos knew I was gone that day and
fucked with me on purpose."

"What? Who told you that?" the Major said, spinning around
in his seat to look at Fahdi.

"He did. Santos admitted it was payback for making fun of
him."

"That little fucker! He could have gotten you killed!" Major
Warren bellowed with anger. "I'm going to fuck him up!"

"No, please don't say anything," Fahdi said shaking his head.
"I promised I wouldn't tell you. The last thing I need is to be
seen as a rat or I really will end up dead out there."

"That's not how Marines treat their brothers! I don't give a
shit what anyone says or thinks, you are one of us."

"Honestly, sir, I am over it. He apologized and I really don't think he knew or understood his actions. He didn't know they'd send me away from the base. He thought they would hold me at the guard shack."

"Allen, this is serious! Are you sure you don't want to pursue any official action against Sergeant Santos? You have every right to do so."

"I'm sure. Really."

The team had the next day off and the guys invited Fahdi to go to the rec room with them to play some video games. A few minutes after arriving at the rec room, Fahdi noticed Sergeant Santos was missing and asked Sergeant Ramirez where he was. Ramirez said the Major needed Santos to meet a local visitor at the main gate. The team often had locals, typically contractors or community leaders, come to the base to discuss current projects and, of course, someone from the team would always have to meet them at the main gate to escort them onto the base. Since these locals rarely spoke any English, the Major usually needed Fahdi to join him in their meetings to translate. Fahdi rushed out of the rec room and over to the Civil Affairs tent, fearing he was supposed to be at the meeting and had simply forgotten about it.

Entering the tent, he was surprised to find the Major lounging on his cot in his PT shorts and a t-shirt. Considering the Major always met visitors wearing his full uniform, Fahdi was confused.

"They guys told me we had a visitor coming in today. Do you need me to translate?" Fahdi asked.

"Nope," Major Warren replied nonchalantly. "No one is coming today."

"Then who is Sergeant Santos waiting for at the gate?"

"Nobody," the Major said with a smile.

Before Fahdi could say anything, Sergeant Santos' voice came over Major Warren's radio. "Sir, wasn't this guy supposed to be here an hour ago? Maybe he's not gonna show. You want me to come back to the tent?"

The Major rolled over and picked up his radio. "Nope, maintain your post, Sergeant. I need you there until he shows. He's probably running late." Warren plopped the radio back on the ground next to his cot.

Fahdi knew what was going on. "How long has he been up there?"

"A couple of hours." The Major looked at his watch. "Whew, it's getting damn hot out there by now, too," he added flippantly.

"I appreciate it, sir, but you didn't have to do this."

"Yes, I did. And the next time something like this happens you better tell me—immediately."

"Yes, sir."

"Now go away. I need to get back to my nap."

Sergeant Santos stood at the main gate waiting for the phantom visitor from 9 a.m. to approximately 3 p.m. that day. Unlike Fahdi, Santos had been allowed to wait in a safe area inside the gate, but there was no escaping the sun. Six hours, full gear, July Iraqi sun—payback's a bitch.

CHAPTER THIRTEEN

SHIT HAPPENS

AUGUST 2004

One morning in early August, Major Warren asked Fahdi if he'd be willing to help out an Army unit for a couple of days whose regular translator had recently quit. Of course, Fahdi agreed. Sergeant Goldberg drove him up to the main gate to meet the unit's convoy, which was prepping to head out for the day to patrol the area.

Fahdi reported to the unit commander, a Lieutenant Colonel Sexton, and informed him he'd be serving as his translator for the next few days. The Lieutenant Colonel spoke with Fahdi for a few minutes asking him a little about his previous experience working for the U.S. military. Fahdi could tell Sexton was simply trying to gauge his English-speaking skills, but was very polite and Fahdi immediately liked him.

A larger convoy, approximately fifteen vehicles, Fahdi was assigned to ride with several soldiers in one of the Humvees near the center of the convoy. As usual, he got to sit in the middle of the backseat.

"The Humvee had a .50 cal mounted to the roof and a soldier manning the turret. The dude's ass was in my face the entire day, but that wasn't the worst part. What really sucked was when the guy had to pee. Of course, we didn't pull over. We had to do the typical piss-in-a-water-bottle routine, and he wasn't even allowed to come down from the turret. One of the other soldiers would pass a water bottle up to him. The first time he had to pee, we were bouncing along down a rough dirt road and he's trying to work around forty pounds of body armor, to hit an opening the size of a nickel, while balancing up in the turret. Needless to say, I got wet. I did my best to ignore it and act like I didn't notice, but there was no way the other soldiers were going to let me off the hook that easily. 'Now you know why we let you sit in the middle,' they kidded, then called me 'piss face' for the rest of the day."

The convoy spent the day merely trolling around the area. They'd stop every now and then and the Lieutenant Colonel would have Fahdi translate while he talked with some locals, but the unit didn't seem to have any solid objective other than ride around and make sure nothing suspicious was going on in the area.

The convoy turned back to head for the base in late afternoon. Fahdi noticed they took a shortcut via a small side road that cut through an open field instead of following the main road back to camp. Narrow, barely wide enough to accommodate the convoy's vehicles, and built up quite a bit with steep banks that dropped off on either side, Fahdi didn't like the lack of mobility the road offered. The vehicles couldn't have turned around if they needed to and one wrong move over the side would spell disaster. He had a bad feeling.

Suddenly they heard it. The distinct thwomp of an RPG being fired off and whistling through the air. Everyone in Fahdi's Humvee braced for impact. A couple of seconds later, there was a massive BOOM! right under the vehicle. The insurgents aimed for their Humvee because it was traveling near the center of the convoy, which is typically where high-ranking officers would be riding. But it just so happened, the Lieutenant Colonel was riding in the very first vehicle of the convoy that day. Luckily, though, the RPG missed the Humvee. The insurgents had aimed a little too low and hit the embankment of the road right under the passenger side of the vehicle.

"It tore the road all to shit, but our Humvee wasn't damaged too badly. We'd have probably all been fine if the driver hadn't panicked. He was just an eighteen-year-old kid who'd been in country for only a few weeks and when he heard the explosion he freaked out. He jerked the wheel, lost control, and over the side of the road we went. The Humvee flipped down the steep bank. All I remember thinking was, *After all I've survived, I'm going to die in a fucking car wreck.*"

The Humvee finally came to a stop completely upside-down and the massive radio box had dislodged from its harness and landed directly on Fahdi's left arm. To make matters worse, the soldier who'd been up in the .50 cal turret was now lying on top of the radio box. Fahdi was pinned and he knew his arm was broken, but in that moment, it was the least of his worries. He feared the insurgents would try to rush the vehicle and slaughter them all before they could get out.

Thank goodness it had been a "fire-and-run" assault. None of the other vehicles were hit and no other attacks followed the single RPG round that took out Fahdi's vehicle.

Before the dust settled, the other soldiers in the convoy rushed down the bank and surrounded the disabled vehicle.

Several immediately started trying to open the doors of the vehicle while others hollered, asking if everyone inside was okay. No one was injured, except Fahdi.

From his position, the gunner had a clear view of Fahdi's face and could see it was twisted in pain. "Hey man, are you okay?" he asked.

"My arm hurts," Fahdi responded through clenched teeth.

The gunner moved to get out of the vehicle, but as he shifted his weight it put more pressure on Fahdi's arm.

"Don't fucking move! You're crushing my arm!" Fahdi cried out in pain.

"That's because my weight is on it. Let me move and they'll be able to get you out." As slowly and carefully as possible, the gunner maneuvered himself off the radio box and slipped into the front area of the vehicle, then pulled the radio off Fahdi's arm. No longer pinned, Fahdi tried to open the door closest to him, but it wouldn't budge.

The soldiers on the outside managed to get the front driver's side door open and pulled the driver and gunner out. They were then able to finally get the back-passenger door open and asked Fahdi if he could move. He couldn't maneuver enough to wriggle himself out without using both arms. His left arm completely useless, Fahdi was stuck. The soldiers grabbed him by the feet and carefully dragged him out of the vehicle on his back. He cradled his arm as the soldiers propped him up against the Humvee. The convoy's medic came over and pulled up the sleeve of Fahdi's uniform top. His lower arm was red and already swelling up. Certain the arm was broken, the medic applied a splint and Fahdi returned to base with half the convoy. The other half stayed behind until a Bradley tank arrived to tow the wrecked Humvee back to the base. The convoy dropped Fahdi off at the TQ Airbase hospital where they x-rayed his arm. Sure enough, his lower left arm was fractured in two places, but they were clean breaks and nothing had to be reset. They put him in a cast up to his elbow that he had to wear for a few weeks, gave him a bottle of Vicodin, and sent him on his way. His arm throbbing unmercifully, Fahdi skipped dinner, popped two pain pills, and went straight to bed. He didn't even stop by the Civil Affairs tent to tell them what had happened.

The next morning, Fahdi awoke to a loud pounding on his trailer door. He groggily glanced at his watch. *Ten o'clock! Damn, those Vicodin are good.* He stumbled to the door to find Major Warren with a concerned look on his face.

"I only found out this morning what happened," the Major said. "Are you okay?"

"Yes, nothing serious, just a broken arm."

Major Warren happened to bump into Lt. Col. Sexton at the chow hall that morning who asked him how his translator was doing after his injury. From the look on the Major's face, Sexton realized he had no clue what he was talking about and filled him in on the previous day's attack.

"He told me you were the only one injured," Major Warren said, stepping into Fahdi's room. "I asked him where you were and he said the last he knew his men had dropped you at the hospital at TQ. I've spent the last two hours over there looking for you. Someone finally told me you'd broken your arm and they'd sent you off with a cast yesterday evening. Why didn't you come tell me what happened last night after you left the hospital?"

"You thought I left for good, didn't you?" Fahdi said with a wily smile.

"No . . . maybe. Well, it did cross my mind," the Major finally admitted. "Allen, I am so sorry this happened to you. I promise I won't loan you out to anyone else while you're assigned to our unit."

"Don't worry about it, sir." Then, excited to utilize a new phrase he'd picked up from the Marines, Fahdi added, "Shit happens."

"Rest up for the next few days. Come by the tent when you think you're ready to come back to work. Do you need anything?"

Fahdi held up and shook his bottle of Vicodin. "These are awesome. You think Goldberg could score me some more?"

Major Warren smiled. "I'll see to it that Goldberg stops by with some more before the end of the day."

In significant pain the first two days, Fahdi spent most of the time locked in his trailer doped up on his pain meds. By day three, the pain had subsided a bit but he was nowhere near ready to go out on any missions with the team. He was, however, getting really bored and decided to head over to the Civil Affairs tent for a change of scenery. The team was in for the day so all the guys were present to welcome Fahdi back when he showed up and sign his cast.

"I should have known better than to set those assholes loose with a permanent marker on my cast," Fahdi said, flashing a nostalgic smile. "I spent the next three weeks with drawings of multiple hairy dicks and sets of balls on my arm."

Major Warren felt bad about what happened to Fahdi and let him use his satellite phone again to call and talk to his family that afternoon. Fahdi got ahold of his brother Fareed and asked how things were going at home. He also told him about his failed attempt to come back for a visit, but did not mention his recent injuries. Once Fahdi had been reassured everything was going okay on the home front, his brother shared some interesting news. Their neighbor Waleed, who'd told Fahdi to flee the Island Palace as Baghdad was falling to the Americans, had landed a position within Iraq's new

National Intelligence Service (INIS) the U.S. had established and was working to rebuild in the Green Zone. Waleed told Fareed the Americans were actively looking for and hiring people to work at the new agency and he'd already managed to get Fareed a job interview. He also informed him they were especially in need of good translators, preferably those who had experience working with the U.S. military throughout Iraq.

"I think he'll be able to get you a job interview if you're interested," Fareed told Fahdi. "I know you told me not to tell anyone that you work for the Americans, but honestly, he already knew what you were doing. I'm sure he won't say anything anyway, considering he's now in just as deep with the U.S. as you are, and it looks like I'm about to be as well. My interview at the INIS was a couple of days ago. I think it went well."

Fahdi remained silent, although his mind was running about a million miles an hour. He didn't want to abandon Major Warren and the Civil Affairs team, but he was worn out and tired of dodging bullets, IEDs, RPGs, and more in Western Iraq. He'd been working six days a week, on seemingly an endless deployment with the U.S. military in Iraq, for nearly eighteen months. He needed a break, plus he was homesick.

As if hearing his brother's thoughts, Fareed broke the silence. "Think about it man, it's a desk job *and* it's here in Baghdad—not just in Baghdad, but inside the Green Zone. You get to come home every night. Plus, they are paying translators $800 a month starting out, $200 more than you're making now. And we all miss you. You being out there is practically killing mom."

After another long pause Fahdi finally said, "Tell him to get me an interview."

"Okay, I'll talk to him tonight," Fareed said excitedly. "When

VOICING THE EAGLE

should I tell him to set it up for? How will you make it back to Baghdad?"

"Just tell him to schedule the interview. I'll figure out the rest."

"Okay. Can you call me back in a couple of days? I should have the info for you by then."

After hanging up with his brother, Fahdi returned the sat phone to Major Warren and told him he needed to talk. Fahdi reluctantly laid out his plan and, to Fahdi's delight, Major Warren was completely supportive.

"This sounds like a fantastic opportunity, Allen. I think you could do this country a lot of good working for the government back in Baghdad," the Major said. "I'll even type you up a reference letter. Let me know if there is anything else I can do to help you out."

Two days later, Fahdi called his brother back. Waleed, had come through on his promise to get Fahdi an interview and Fareed passed along the date and time. It was in two weeks. All Fahdi had to do was figure out how to make it back to Baghdad—alive. Fahdi relayed the news to Major Warren, along with his reservations regarding how he'd make it to Baghdad for the interview and then back to the base afterwards. He wouldn't know if he'd be hired until at least six weeks after the interview due to the extensive background checks the U.S. was conducting on all the new employees, so he didn't want to quit his Titan job until he knew for sure he had a new job to roll into. His plan was to return and continue working with the Civil Affairs team until officially offered a position at the INIS.

Major Warren silently mulled over Fahdi's predicament for a few minutes. "If I can get you to BIAP will you be able to get where you need to be on your own from there?"

"Yes, as long as I'm in Baghdad, I'll be fine. I can handle the rest."

"Okay, let me make some phone calls and I'll get back with you."

"I really appreciate it, sir."

Two days later, Major Warren informed Fahdi he'd arranged for the two of them to take a military chopper flight to Baghdad the day before Fahdi's scheduled interview at the INIS and then fly back to the base the morning after his interview.

Fahdi later found out the Major had scheduled a "bogus" meeting he had to attend in Baghdad and needed his translator to accompany him.

Over the next week, leading up to their flight to Baghdad, the Major would joke around with Fahdi whenever they'd be preparing for their daily patrols, saying things like, "Now don't you go and get yourself killed before landing your cushy new desk job!"

"It's not a job yet, just an interview."

CHAPTER FOURTEEN

I'VE HAD ENOUGH

SEPTEMBER 2004

Fahdi and Major Warren landed at Baghdad International Airport the afternoon before Fahdi's INIS interview. Before getting off the chopper, Major Warren put a hand on Fahdi's shoulder. "We fly back at 0800 the day after tomorrow. Make sure you're back here in time to catch the chopper."

Fahdi nodded.

"Are you coming back?" Major Warren asked solemnly.

"Yes, I'll be here," Fahdi reassured him.

"Don't lie to me, Allen. If you don't plan on coming back, it's okay. Just tell me."

"Don't worry, sir. I'll be back. I give you my word."

"If anything changes or you run into any problems, call me on my sat phone."

Fahdi had no clue what the Major did for those two days in Baghdad. All he knew was there was no "meeting" he had to attend.

Not wanting to deal with the drama of a family reunion the evening before his big interview, Fahdi had Waleed pick him up from BIAP. Fahdi stayed at his house that night and then he drove Fahdi to the INIS building the following morning for his interview.

They sat in silence for the first ten minutes on the drive from the airport.

Unable to hold back any longer, Waleed looked at Fahdi, and simply asked, "How long?"

He knows. "A long time," Fahdi replied quietly.

"Are you okay?" Waleed asked, glancing at the cast on Fahdi's arm.

"Yeah."

Fahdi planned to bust the cast off that night, not wanting to show up for his interview with it on.

"Where have you been working? Everyone knows you haven't been in Baghdad."

"I've been in Al-Anbar for the past six months."

"What? Are you insane?"

"That's what everyone keeps telling me."

Fahdi's INIS interview lasted about two hours. They asked very little about his skills or employment experience and a lot about his background: what school did he attend, what did his father do for a living, what did his grandfathers do for a living, where has he lived, etc. They also had Fahdi's Titan employee file with all the information in it from the background check the company did. The INIS interviewer even asked Fahdi some of the same questions right out of the file to see if his answers would differ at all from those he'd given Titan six months prior.

Fahdi felt confident during the interview, all the questions were straightforward, but he had no idea if he'd done well enough to land the job. The interviewer did not give any hints one way or the other.

After the interview, he went home to visit his mom. Surprised by his unannounced visit, she cried tears of joy for the first hour, then she spent the rest of the evening begging him not to return. She kept asking him if he was participating in any dangerous missions and if he really was okay. He lied, insisting he was working a boring desk job, but a mother knows. She could see the stress etched across her son's face. He'd visibly aged ten years and she knew in her heart Fahdi was anything but "fine."

To help alleviate her worries and give her at least a spark of hope, he told her about his interview and the opportunity at the INIS.

After calming her down, he picked up the phone and started calling various friends—classmates from college, neighborhood buddies, old primary school friends, etc. He wanted to spread word of his return from Mosul to reinforce the cover story his family had been promulgating during his absence. He even invited one of his closest friends from school, whom he'd known since kindergarten, to stop by the house that evening to catch up.

Sitting on the living room couch sipping *chai*, Fahdi's friend asked him point blank, "Fahdi, where have you been?"

"I told you, I've been in Mosul working with my uncles."

"Don't lie to me. Everyone knows," his friend replied glumly.

"What do you mean?" Fahdi tried his best to keep up the front.

"You know exactly what I mean Let's not play this game. No, I don't want you to tell me where you've been. I'd rather not know. But I'm telling you for your own sake, quit now. We're friends and I love you. Please stop working for them. Everyone around here knows what you're doing. It's not safe. You know what they do to people like you."

Fahdi spent most of the night lying awake in bed, seriously considering not returning to the airport the next morning to meet the Major, but he'd given his word. He felt like he had very little control left over his own life. Choosing not to sacrifice his honor was one of the few things he *could* control.

Major Warren also had serious doubts Fahdi would return and was visibly surprised when Fahdi showed up at the airport the next morning. "You really came back," the Major quipped with a smile as Fahdi approached.

"I told you I would," Fahdi replied straight-faced. "Yeah, but I know how it is. I figured after you saw your family and home you wouldn't be able to fly back into hell with me. Why did you come back?"

"I won't lie, I definitely considered not showing up this morning. But my honor seems to be one of the few things I have left in this world, so here I am."

After Fahdi and Major Warren returned from their three-day jaunt to Baghdad, the Civil Affairs Unit resumed their usual missions. Two weeks later, the Major blindsided Fahdi with the news the team would be relocating in a few days to Southern Iraq to carry out the final month of their deployment before returning to the U.S. Fahdi wasn't familiar with the southern part of the country and had no friends or connections in the area. If there was any kind of emergency or if he simply had to make his way back to Baghdad on his own once the Major returned to the U.S., his resources would be extremely limited. He also expressed to Major Warren his concerns that the area they were relocating to was a stronghold for extremist Shia

Cleric Muqtada Al-Sadr, whose Shiite militia, the Mahdi Army, was rapidly gaining strength and power across the southern provinces of Iraq.

"Those guys are psycho," Fahdi said, regarding Al-Sadr's militia.

"It's not like it's any better out here," Major Warren replied. "The assholes in Al-Qaeda aren't exactly known for their balanced rationale."

"Well, as we say here in Iraq, the 'crazy' you know and are familiar with is better than the 'crazy' you don't know."

Fahdi was extremely bummed about the team's relocation. He hoped his new job at the INIS would come through before the Civil Affairs Unit returned to the U.S. The last thing he wanted was to be left behind floundering and having to work for God-knows-who while he waited, but transferring with the team was too risky. The southern part of the country was practically a foreign country to Fahdi and his skills as Major Warren's translator would be subpar for the region. When it came to Northern and Western Iraq, he knew the lay of the land, had connections, and, most importantly, knew how to read the people. He'd be at a disadvantage in the south that could possibly prove detrimental to both himself and the team.

Fahdi asked Major Warren for one last favor before he left: could he arrange for Fahdi to be transferred back to the Iraqi Army training camp where he could translate for the American drill instructors. Fahdi desperately needed a break from combat missions. Tired of getting shot at, he was, above all, fed up with IEDs. Additionally, after working with the Civil Affairs team for so long, he honestly didn't trust anyone else to watch his back out in the field nor did he have the energy or desire to start all over as the "new guy" with a brand-new unit.

Major Warren happily obliged Fahdi's request. The day before the Civil Affairs team transferred south, Fahdi returned to Camp Ar-Ramadi and the Iraqi Army boot camp.

"That was a tough day," Fahdi recalled somberly. "It was really hard leaving those guys, knowing I'd probably never see them again, which I haven't. I can't believe that was twelve years ago. It feels like yesterday. I've stayed in contact with a couple of them via email and Facebook. As far as I know, everyone made it home safe from Iraq, but I haven't seen any of them in person since the day I transferred back to Ramadi."

CHAPTER FIFTEEN

WE ARE ALL FUCKED

SEPTEMBER 2004

At Camp Ar-Ramadi, Fahdi reported to Captain Rowe, who was still in charge of running the Iraqi Army boot camp, now officially known as the Iraqi National Guard (ING). Fahdi missed his Marine brothers but was looking forward to some relative peace and quiet.

Fahdi was amazed by the extensive transformation that had taken place on the training side of the base since he'd left. Several new structures had been erected, including barracks for the Iraqi soldiers, offices, and storage buildings for the ING's weapons and equipment. What had been nothing more than a couple of shacks and an obstacle course in the middle of a huge field had metamorphosed into a legitimate military base over the past six months.

Captain Rowe was one of the few familiar faces that remained at Camp Ar-Ramadi. Sergeant Benning and his team had rotated back to the states a few months after Fahdi left. There were a couple new American drill sergeants at the camp, but they no longer actively trained the new recruits. The ING had their own training instructors now. The U.S. drill instructors simply served as advisors and helped Captain Rowe oversee the training camp. Fahdi recognized a couple of the Iraqi soldiers now serving as drill sergeants as those who'd gone through boot camp at the time he was translating for Benning. Advancement from recruit to drill sergeant can be highly accelerated when your military is technically only eighteen months old.

The next day, Fahdi reported for duty to Captain Rowe's office. Upon seeing Fahdi, the Captain broke into a wide smile and pushed himself up from his desk.

"I heard you had an exciting tour with the Marines over there in Fallujah," Captain Rowe said as he offered Fahdi a handshake.

"Yes, sir. I learned a lot."

"There's a glowing Letter of Recommendation for you laying on my desk from a Captain Warren. Whatever you did, you definitely made an impression. How would you like to work directly for me?"

"I'd love to, sir," Fahdi replied. "But in the spirit of full disclosure, I don't know how much longer I'll be a translator with Titan."

Fahdi brought Captain Rowe up to speed regarding his recent INIS interview and explained he was simply biding his time in Ramadi to see if his new job panned out. Rowe told Fahdi he'd be heading back to the U.S. himself in a couple of months anyway and the timing would work out perfectly.

By the second day of his new gig as Captain Rowe's personal translator, Fahdi was extremely content with his position. In fact, he hoped the INIS would take their time in getting back to him about the job.

"Working for Captain Rowe was a nine-to-five desk job. I rarely had to do anything. I just sat in his office all day and, every now and then, I'd translate between the Captain and the Iraqi drill instructors. By that time, the Captain had everything within the training camp running efficiently and he spent most the day either working out or eating. While he was at the gym, I chilled in his office. Another great bonus was every day for lunch the Captain ordered a big platter of Iraqi food from a local restaurant one of the Iraqi officers would bring to our office. I think I gained a good ten or fifteen pounds in the two months I worked for him.

"Then after lunch Captain Rowe would have me sit at his desk while he took a nap on his office couch. After spending every day of the last few months fearing for my life, working for Captain Rowe was a dream come true. But even though I was finally able to relax, and Captain Rowe really gave me the hook-up, I missed Major Warren and the guys from the Civil Affairs team. They had become my friends, more than my friends, and I felt alone again."

Soon, the entire training camp, including Fahdi and his newfound tranquility, would be severely rocked by a major scandal merely two weeks into Fahdi's cushy new assignment.

During this time, the Iraqi National Guard soldiers were being paid directly by the U.S. military in U.S. currency. The local ING members stationed at the base collected their salaries directly from Captain Rowe and his staff. Twice a month, a Marine Sergeant carrying a military backpack stuffed with cash—similar to the backpack the Civil Affairs team carried around paying out reparations in Fallujah—would sit in the office next-door to Captain Rowe's and spend an entire day distributing the money to hundreds of Iraqi soldiers as they filed one-by-one into the office. It was typically an efficient process as each soldier's money was inside a sealed envelope with his name on the front and the envelopes were alphabetized. On one particular payday, for whatever reason, the Marine Sergeant showed up with the cash all loose in the bag, not divided into the envelopes. The Sergeant explained to Captain Rowe that when he'd arrived at HQ earlier that morning to retrieve the money bag, there'd been a delay, and by the time he signed for the bag, he didn't have time to get everything divvied up before leaving for the office to hand out the salaries. Considering there was about $350,000 floating around in the bag that needed to be properly distributed to hundreds of soldiers, Captain Rowe knew there was no way one Marine Sergeant would get it all done in a single day, so Captain Rowe called in the Iraqi Brigade Commander and two Iraqi soldiers to help the Marine pass out the salaries.

"The two soldiers Captain Rowe had helping were young guys, no more than eighteen or nineteen, who worked as Captain Rowe's office assistants. Their daily duties consisted of cleaning the Captain's office, running errands for him, bringing him food, etc. Captain Rowe knew these kids pretty well and since they were so young he assumed he wouldn't have to worry about them being ballsy enough to mess with the money. But I'm sure you can already guess what happened."

Even with the added task of having to count out all the salaries on the spot, the morning salary distributions went smoothly. Captain Rowe checked on the progress at lunchtime and the Marine Sergeant happily informed him they were only slightly behind schedule; confident they'd get everything done by early evening at the latest.

A couple of hours after lunch, Captain Rowe and Fahdi were in the Captain's office doing some paperwork when the Marine Sergeant stormed in, practically ripping the office door off its hinges. "The bag is gone!" he shrieked in a tone Fahdi had never heard emanate from a Marine's mouth.

"What bag is gone?" Captain Rowe asked, though he knew full well what bag the Sergeant was referring to but was desperate to delay the inevitable.

"The money bag, sir," he blurted out in between spurts of hyperventilation. "I went to the bathroom and left the two Iraqi soldiers with it for just a minute, and when I came back, both of them and the money bag were gone! Oh, my God! I'm going to throw up!"

"Fahdi, get on the radio and tell the gate guards to stop those sons-of-bitches!"

Fahdi jumped on the radio and relayed to the Iraqi soldiers on duty at the gate to intercept the two fugitive soldiers. He passed along their names and descriptions, but the guards radioed back the men had exited the base minutes before.

"Fuck!" Captain Rowe screamed, able to understand enough Arabic to discern the message the gate guards had relayed before Fahdi translated. "What about the Commander, where is he?" Captain Rowe roared at the Marine Sergeant.

"He wasn't in the office when I stepped out to go to the bathroom. I think he went outside for a smoke," the Marine answered, nearly in tears.

"Fahdi, go find the Commander!" the Captain screamed.

Fahdi raced out of the office, relieved to get out of the room, certain Captain Rowe was about to disembowel the Marine Sergeant then and there. As Fahdi ran down the hallway, he heard the Captain release a steady stream of obscenities as he laid into the Marine.

Fahdi found the Iraqi Commander outside near the smoke shack finishing up a cigarette. Either the Commander was an extremely skilled actor or genuinely oblivious to the shit storm erupting inside. Fahdi yelled to the Commander he needed to come with him right away and the two sprinted to Captain Rowe's office. Before opening the office door Fahdi could hear the Captain still chewing out the Marine, who was now crumpled to the floor with his head in his hands.

"How much fucking money was left in the bag Sergeant?" Captain Rowe bellowed.

"A little over $200,000, maybe closer to $250,000, sir," the Marine replied sobbing.

"You're a dead man, Sergeant! You're going to be court martialed for this and probably end up in prison because you're fucking stupid! What on God's green Earth could possess you to leave two Iraqi teenagers alone with a bag full of cash? Are you a fucking idiot? Holy fucking God! We are all fucked!"

"I'm sorry! I'm sorry! I'm so, so sorry!" the Sergeant wailed, rocking back and forth.

Captain Rowe caught sight of Fahdi and the Iraqi Commander standing near the doorway and stormed across the office, making a direct beeline for the Commander. He reached out and grabbed the robust Commander with both hands by the shirt and lifted him off the ground in a rage.

"What did you know about this?" the Captain screamed in the Iraqi Commander's face.

The Commander's eyes popped wide with terror and he shook his head in confusion. The Commander didn't understand any English and Fahdi had yet to debrief him on the situation. He had no idea why Captain Rowe was dangling him six inches off the ground and screaming in his face. Fahdi gave the Commander a quick run-down on what happened and hoped the Commander would have time to answer before the Captain killed him. The Commander swore up and down he had no idea what the young soldiers had done or where they'd gone with the money.

Captain Rowe snarled but released the Commander, convinced he was clueless. With his next breath, he ordered Fahdi to send out a mass radio call in both English and Arabic alerting all American and Iraqi units in the area of the situation and providing a description of the two Iraqi solider suspects. Captain Rowe even had Fahdi announce in Arabic that whoever brought back the missing soldiers and the money bag would receive a $10,000 reward. In a matter of minutes the Iraqi side of the base was deserted. The hunt was on.

An hour after the money went missing, the base Military Police reported to Captain Rowe's office and began their questioning. They started with the Marine Sergeant, then moved on to Captain Rowe, followed by Fahdi. Where were you when the incident occurred? Do you personally know the guys who did this? Do you know where they live?

"They acted like I should've known who these guys were and where they lived simply because I'm Iraqi. I wanted to say, 'Dude, I'm from Baghdad. I don't know these people or where they live. You're American. Do you know every American and where they live?' Of course, I didn't really say this. I was scared shitless we were all going to end up in Abu Ghraib and simply answered their questions as quickly and politely as possible."

The MPs wrapped up their questioning and arrested the Marine Sergeant, escorting him out of the building in handcuffs. Captain Rowe and Fahdi spent the remainder of the afternoon anxiously waiting by the radio for any updates from those out in the field searching for the fugitives. Around 6 p.m., an Iraqi Army unit radioed in they'd apprehended one of the suspects and were en route to the base with him.

"What about the money bag?" Rowe pressed anxiously. Fahdi relayed the Captain's question, but the unit leader came back saying all they'd found on him was $500. And when questioned, he'd said he'd been kicked out of the car by his buddy who took off with the rest of the money.

The unit brought the kid directly to the Captain who had them put him in one of the empty offices, then Rowe and Fahdi went in to interrogate him. The young soldier was scared to death, and rightfully so. The first words out of his mouth were, "It wasn't my idea." Fahdi asked him where his buddy was and, more importantly, where the money was. The kid said they were headed for Fallujah and his friend kicked him out of the car. "I told him we'd made a huge mistake and we were going to get caught," the soldier shrieked hysterically through sobs. "He stopped the car and told me to get out and go home. I didn't know what to do. Then he pulled a gun on me, handed me $500, and forced me out."

Captain Rowe didn't buy the kid's story. The Captain stood up and gave the kid a swift right hook to the cheek, knocking him out of his chair. Rowe smacked the kid around a few more times and even tasered him, but the kid stuck to his story, screaming over and over all he had was $500 and for Captain Rowe to take it.

Satisfied the kid wasn't going to talk, Rowe and Fahdi stepped outside the room to regroup. The Iraqi Commander—the one Rowe had tossed around like a rag doll earlier—was standing in the hallway outside the room and asked if he could try talking to the kid. Rowe still wasn't convinced the Commander didn't have anything to do with the theft and refused to let him go in to talk to the kid alone. The Commander protested, saying the kid wasn't going to speak with Captain Rowe in the room, but maybe he could make him talk one-on-one. Rowe refused, then relented, stating as long as Fahdi went in to witness the exchange, he would wait in the hallway. The Commander agreed.

The Iraqi Commander questioned the soldier for several minutes, but he, too, failed to get anything useful out of him. As Fahdi and the Iraqi Commander stepped out of the room, they saw the kid's father and two uncles in the hallway with Captain Rowe. Turns out the kid was from a well-off, upper-middle-class family in the area and his dad was a minor Sheikh in the region.

"How much money is missing?" the young soldier's father asked Captain Rowe. "We'll pay it, please just let my son go."

Fahdi informed the family the missing sum was $250,000 and the father's eyes nearly fell out of his head. "Oh, that is an impossible amount," he said dejectedly. "May I at least speak to my son? Perhaps I can reason with him."

Rowe allowed the family to go in and talk to the soldier, again under the condition Fahdi accompany them to witness the conversation. The father and uncles spent the next ten minutes screaming at the kid. Then they, too, started beating on him. Captain Rowe overheard the ruckus from the hallway and burst into the room. By the time Captain Rowe pulled the family off of him, the kid had a couple broken ribs and a concussion.

"I did not raise him this way!" the father screamed as Captain Rowe and Fahdi dragged him and his brothers out of the room. "He's my only son and now he's dead to us. This is going to kill his mother. What will happen to him? Will he go to Abu Ghraib?"

Captain Rowe felt sorry for the father, but all he could tell him was the kid's fate was in no way up to him.

Midnight rolled around and there was no word of the other missing soldier. Fahdi told the Captain it was a lost cause. The kid was long gone.

"It's not a lost cause. We will have everyone resume the search at first light," Rowe persisted.

"Look, $250,000 is a *lot* of money around here," Fahdi explained. "I could have been to Canada by now. We're not far from the border and there are underground routes all over this place. Hand one of the border agents in Syria a $1,000 and not only will he get you across the border, he'll suck your dick once you're on the other side. Trust me, the money is gone. I bet you anything it's no longer on Iraqi soil."

At dawn, the MPs showed up to collect the kid, whose face was so swollen and caked with blood, mainly from the beating his family had given him, the MPs had no choice but to question Captain Rowe and Fahdi about his injuries.

"We didn't touch him," Captain Rowe fibbed. "His own family did this to him. Go ahead, ask him. Fahdi will translate for you."

When the MPs went into the room to examine the soldier, Captain Rowe quietly said to Fahdi, "If he says I even laid a finger on him, you make damn sure that doesn't get translated."

Fahdi's stomach sank. He wasn't prepared to lie for Captain Rowe, but nodded anyway and secretly prayed the kid wouldn't accuse the Captain. Much to Fahdi's relief, when the MPs asked the soldier who'd beaten him, he laid it all on his family. The MPs gave Captain Rowe a bit of a tongue lashing for allowing the family to beat the kid, but that was the extent of it.

A few days later the detained Iraqi soldier's family showed back up to the base and asked to speak to Captain Rowe, saying they had information regarding the whereabouts of the missing soldier who'd taken off with the money. They led Captain Rowe to their car parked outside the gate on the Iraqi side of the base where they had one of the missing kid's uncles practically tied up in the backseat of the car.

"What the hell is this?" Captain Rowe shouted in confusion.

"This is the missing boy's uncle," the father of the detained soldier announced proudly.

"I don't need his fucking uncle!" Captain Rowe hissed. "I need *him* and my goddamn money!"

"Question him. He knows where the kid is," the father pressed.

Captain Rowe bent down and looked through the open back window of the car. "Do you know where your nephew is?" he asked and Fahdi translated.

"No."

"See," Captain Rowe said to the desperate father. "A waste of my fucking time. Don't bother coming back unless you have the missing kid or the missing money. Those are the only two things that will get your son released."

"The incident sparked a war between those two families that got vicious from what information seeped into the camp over the next couple of weeks. Out of revenge for their son being locked up, the family of the soldier Rowe had in custody killed a cousin of the kid that escaped, and then of course, that family had to avenge the cousin's death and went after some innocent young guy in the other family, and on and on. There were at least two confirmed deaths and God only knows what else. Those two families are probably plotting against each other to this day. All because of a bag of America money."

CHAPTER SIXTEEN

I QUIT

OCTOBER 2004

Since his return to Ramadi, Fahdi had been borrowing Captain Rowe's satellite phone every couple of days to call his neighbor Waleed and ask if he'd landed the position at the INIS. Whenever the INIS made a formal job offer, new employees had to report to the building within seven days to accept the offer in person. Since there was no way for anyone to get a hold of Fahdi in an American camp, he put Waleed's phone number as his contact number, then called and checked in every few days. Fahdi feared the process was taking too long and began to accept the reality he probably wasn't going to get the job.

His hopes were renewed in mid-September. Waleed reported Fahdi's brother had been hired and that if his brother passed the security check, chances were good he'd be hired as well.

Finally, one day in early October, Fahdi made his usual call to check in with Waleed and was given the news he'd been waiting for.

"You're hired!" Waleed practically screeched into the phone as soon as he answered Fahdi's call. "Now get your ass back to Baghdad, ASAP! Your approval came through two days ago. I managed to buy you a few extra days by telling them you were in Ramadi working with the Americans, but you have to report by next Friday to accept in person or they will cancel the offer."

Fahdi hung up the phone and made a beeline for Captain Rowe's office. He handed the Captain his phone and told him the news. Captain Rowe was aware of Fahdi's pending application at the INIS and, although he wasn't happy about losing his translator, he congratulated Fahdi and wished him the best of luck in his new position. All Fahdi had to do now was figure out how to make it back to Baghdad in one piece.

"Sir, is there any way you could perhaps hook me up with a seat on a Baghdad bound chopper?" Fahdi asked Captain Rowe.

"I'll see what I can do. When do you plan on heading out?"

"As soon as possible; tomorrow or the next day would be great."

"Well, it'll take me at least three days to arrange for you to fly out on a chopper. There is a convoy heading to Baghdad tomorrow. I can probably get you a seat."

"That'd be great, sir. I really appreciate it."

"What about your money?"

The Titan translators collected their salaries from a Titan representative who visited the base the first of each month. Captain Rowe knew the Titan rep was due in the next couple of days to pay Fahdi for his previous month's work. If Fahdi wasn't there to collect, he could kiss the entire month's pay goodbye.

Fahdi shrugged. "I can't wait around for him. If I don't get back to Baghdad and report to the INIS by next Friday, I'll lose the job. I don't want to risk it. After I'm back in Baghdad, I'll stop by Titan headquarters and see if I can collect it there."

Captain Rowe chuckled. "Good luck. That's a long shot, at best. How much do they owe you?"

"My salary is $620 a month, sir."

"I'll give you the money," Captain Rowe replied and opened his bottom desk drawer, which contained a small, locked box.

"Really, sir? Thank you so much!" Fahdi exclaimed. "Wait, can you do that?" he added cautiously, thinking about all the legal issues Captain Rowe just went through over lost money. "Do I need to sign something so the Titan pay manager knows to give the money to you?"

Captain Rowe waved his hand in the air. "No, don't worry about it man. I'll take care of it."

As luck would have it, the convoy Fahdi was supposed to catch a ride on back to Baghdad was unexpectedly postponed at the last minute and rescheduled to depart the following week. Fahdi couldn't wait that long; he'd have to figure out a "Plan B." He borrowed Captain Rowe's satellite phone and called up his friend from Ramadi, the same one who'd given him a ride back to Baghdad from Ramadi a few months ago, and asked him if there was any way he could drive Fahdi's car out to him in Ramadi.

"What the hell are you doing back in Ramadi?" his friend asked surprised. "Dude, I don't even go to Ramadi anymore. The road between here and Ramadi is deadly."

Fahdi certainly didn't want to tell him the truth. He proceeded to fabricate a story about how he'd sold his car to a guy in Ramadi and needed someone to drive it out from Baghdad. Sensing his friend's hesitation, he offered him $300 for his trouble. That cinched the deal. His friend promptly agreed to meet Fahdi the next afternoon with his car.

By evening, Fahdi had bought a second-hand .9mm pistol from one of the Iraqi Army officers from the base. No way he was going to make the drive from Ramadi to Baghdad—straight through the infamous triangle of death—alone and completely unarmed.

Fahdi met his friend the next afternoon about a mile from the camp to pick up his car. He dropped his friend off at his parents' house in Ramadi and Fahdi prepped to make the trek to Baghdad solo. Pulling his new pistol out of the waistband of his jeans, he chambered a round and laid the gun on the passenger seat. On the main highway, he laid into the gas pedal of his BMW and assumed a steady 100 mph pace as he headed toward Baghdad.

An hour into his drive, Fahdi noticed a car in his rearview mirror steadily gaining on him. Considering his speed and how fast the mystery car was approaching, Fahdi guessed it had to be pushing 120 mph. As the car got close enough for Fahdi to make out the people inside via his rearview mirror, he knew he was in deep shit. There were at least two men in the car and they had their faces concealed with head scarves.

Fuck.

In all probability, they were road pirates interested in carjacking Fahdi's BMW, but oftentimes a simple vehicle theft in Iraq resulted in the driver being dumped on the side of the road with a bullet in his head.

Fahdi floored it to 125 mph, but could not shake his pursuers. The bandits remained right on his tail. Fahdi took note of the vehicle they were driving, a little white Mitsubishi sedan.

Seriously?

About a mile into what was now an obvious car chase, the passenger of the Mitsubishi stuck an Ak-47 out the window and fired a couple of rounds at Fahdi's car. It was clear they didn't want to damage the car too much and aimed low to try to blow out a tire and disable the vehicle. Fahdi eyeballed his pistol. There was no way he could shoot out the window behind him while driving 120 mph. He decided his only option was to keep driving, as long as possible, in hopes of eventually outrunning or outlasting them.

After a few minutes, Fahdi had managed to put a little distance between him and the hijackers, but they were still in hot pursuit. Then, ahead on the horizon, Fahdi saw a U.S. military convoy that appeared to be parked on the side of the road. He felt a bit of relief for a second, but quickly realized he was now between a rock and hard place. Barreling up on a U.S. convoy at 120 mph was a good way to get your car sliced in half by a hail of fire from a couple .50 cals, but it wasn't like slowing down was an option. He had to attract the attention of the convoy before he got too close or the guys behind him managed to shoot out his tires. Fahdi had an idea, a really bad idea, but there was no other choice. He grabbed his .9mm, stuck it out his window, and fired off a couple of shots aimed at the back of the convoy's rear Humvee. As soon as the first round was heard, the soldiers of the convoy scrambled to train the .50 cals in Fahdi's direction. He slammed on the brakes, stopping in the middle of the road, jumped out with his hands held high in the sky, and began walking toward the convoy.

The bandits had seen Fahdi open fire on the American convoy and the soldiers begin to mobilize. In a cloud of dust, they whipped their truck around in a tight U-turn and sped away in the opposite direction.

Fahdi was relieved, but it was extremely short-lived. He had only jumped from the frying pan into the fire.

Approximately 100 yards from the convoy, Fahdi halted his approach and stood in the middle of the road with his hands on his head. A handful of soldiers jogged toward him with their M-16s trained on his chest. The team leader screamed at Fahdi to lay face-down on the ground and spread his arms. Fahdi complied. The soldiers surrounded Fahdi and one placed his knee on Fahdi's back while he zip-tied Fahdi's hands behind him. They stood him up, frisked him for weapons and then half drug him back to the convoy.

Reaching the convoy, the soldiers pushed Fahdi to the ground beside one of the Humvees. Fahdi remained silent, knowing it would be a waste of time to say anything until face to face with a ranking officer in the convoy. A few minutes later, three soldiers approached. The one in the middle yelled, "Someone find my terp." Fahdi scanned the man's uniform, an Army Captain.

High enough.

"Sir, I speak English," Fahdi said meekly.

"Oh, well congratulations," the Captain replied sarcastically. "Then how about you use your English to tell me why the fuck you were firing at my convoy?"

Fahdi explained the situation to the Captain, told him he was a Titan translator, and rattled off all the names and numbers of the military units he'd worked for. He also told the Captain if he looked in the glovebox of his car, he'd find his Titan badge and letters of recommendation from Captain Rowe and Major Warren.

The Captain and his men spent the next hour searching Fahdi's car and making several calls to confirm his story and identity. For once, Fahdi's unique looks paid off. Everyone always remembered the green-eyed Iraqi terp.

Confident of Fahdi's loyalties, the Captain ordered one of his soldiers to cut Fahdi's hands loose. "I'm going to have to confiscate your pistol," the Captain said half-apologetically. "I can't allow you to keep a weapon that's been discharged at U.S. forces. It's simply policy."

"I understand, sir."

"You're trying to get to Baghdad?"

"Yes, sir," Fahdi replied with a nod.

"Well, you're welcome to tag along behind us in your car. We're headed for BIAP."

Perfect. "Thank you so much, sir," Fahdi said gratefully. "I really appreciate it." Then it occurred to him, driving into Baghdad as a blatant part of an American convoy probably wasn't the best idea. "Sir, if you don't mind," Fahdi added, "I'll keep a little distance between myself and the convoy, if that's okay with you."

"What, are you ashamed to be seen with us?" the Captain replied harshly.

"Well, no . . . of course not," Fahdi stammered. "I mean no disrespect . . . it's just that . . . well . . ."

The Captain cut him off with a loud belly laugh. "I'm fucking with you, kid. It's okay. I get it. Stay as far back as you want, but remember, the farther away you are, the longer it'll take us to save your ass should you run into any more trouble."

As Fahdi walked over to get in his car, he thought to himself how lucky he was that it'd been an Army convoy he had to shoot at. *If they'd been Marines, I'd be dead.*

As soon as the convoy crossed into a familiar part of Baghdad, Fahdi broke off from the line of vehicles and headed for Waleed's house. His car had taken a couple of rounds to the trunk from the bandit's AK-47 and if he pulled up to his mom's house with bullet holes in his car, she'd probably have a heart attack. He decided to leave it at Waleed's until he could take it to a shop to get patched up.

"I walked into my mom's house and it was like I'd returned from the dead," Fahdi remembered with a smile.

His mom embraced him over and over, and through streaming tears begged him not to return to work for the U.S. military. Much to her joy and relief Fahdi happily informed her he was home for good; that he'd landed a new job at the INIS.

CHAPTER SEVENTEEN

THE INIS

OCTOBER-DECEMBER 2004

The original building housing the Iraqi Intelligence Service under Saddam had been leveled in the war, and the agency had been dissolved by the Coalition.

The newly established agency, now the Iraqi National Intelligence Service (INIS), took over Iraq's former Ministry of Agriculture building. It was one of the few buildings that survived the war with relatively little damage and was also large enough to contain the new Intelligence Service.

Fahdi's first few days at the INIS consisted of a whirlwind of in-processing procedures and paperwork; pages upon pages of forms to fill out. They fingerprinted him and took photos for his ID badges. He also had another brief security interview with an American who was presumably a member of the CIA. No one ever openly mentioned the CIA, but it was common knowledge the INIS was being rebuilt primarily by them. The last thing to do was the polygraph.

"I guess I passed," Fahdi recalled, grinning. "They didn't fire me."

After three days of in-processing, Fahdi hadn't been told what his actual position would be or even what department he'd be assigned to work within.

Walking in on the fourth morning, they simply instructed him to report to the 8th floor of the building; no further details or other info of any kind.

Fahdi stepped off the elevator and practically bumped into a young guy sitting at a rudimentary reception desk stuck in the middle of the hallway right outside the elevator. After asking for his name, the man instructed Fahdi to wait there by the desk and disappeared around the corner. He returned a few minutes later accompanied by an older Iraqi man who was well over six feet tall and dressed in a nice suit.

"Hi, my name is Abu Zaid. You'll be working with us," the older gentlemen said, extending his hand to Fahdi for a Western-style handshake.

"Nice to meet you," Fahdi said, shaking the man's hand.

"Do you know what we do here?" Abu Zaid asked cryptically.

"Not a clue," Fahdi replied shaking his head. "All I know is I was hired as a linguist. My guess is I'll be translating something, but I have no idea what and I don't really care. If it's English, I make it Arabic; if it's Arabic, I make it English, and then I go home every night."

"I like you already. You don't ask questions." Abu Zaid said with a smile, then turned and began walking down the hall. "Come on, let's go meet the big boss. He's been waiting for you."

Abu Zaid led Fahdi into a large office at the end of the hallway furnished with a massive conference table that appeared to have been spit-shined until it gleamed. Another man, also an older Iraqi, was sitting at the far end of the conference table and rose to greet Fahdi and Abu Zaid as they entered the room.

"Ah, you must be Fahdi," the man said with a smile, extending his hand in greeting.

"Yes, sir."

"It's a pleasure to finally meet you. My name is Halil. I am the head of the department you'll be assigned to. Please have a seat," he said, gesturing for Fahdi and Abu Zaid to take seats at the conference table. "We were worried there for a minute you wouldn't make it out of Ramadi. A little trouble on the road, huh?"

"Uhh, well . . . yes. I mean, there was . . ." Fahdi fumbled, trying to figure out if Halil was referring to the incident with the carjackers and Fahdi shooting at the U.S. convoy. And if so, how he would know about it?

Halil and Abu Zaid smiled at each other, apparently amused by Fahdi's confusion. "All that matters is you're here now," Halil said calmly. "I actually requested you personally. I hear you have extensive experience working directly with the American forces in the field and have done much to distinguish yourself as not only a gifted translator but one who doesn't shy away from the more, shall we say, adventurous missions."

"Well, thank you, sir," Fahdi replied with a nervous smile, hoping Halil didn't have plans for him to return to similar work. "But I was kind of hoping to get away from those more 'adventurous missions' by coming to work here."

"Oh, not to worry, your position here will be quite tame. I fear you may find it rather boring being behind a desk for most of the workday."

"No, sir," Fahdi said relieved, "that sounds perfect."

Halil and Abu Zaid took Fahdi on a brief tour of the 8th floor department. As they walked down the hallway, toward the first office, Halil looked to Fahdi and said, "Oh, by the way, your brother works in this department, too. Did he tell you?"

"Nope," Fahdi replied shaking his head, "he hasn't told me anything about his job here, and I don't ask."

"Good boys," Halil said impressed.

The first stop on Fahdi's tour was his future office, the translator room. There were four translators assigned to the department. Fahdi now made five. The linguists worked on two separate shifts, a day shift and an evening shift. Halil introduced Fahdi to the two translators currently on duty and informed him he'd start out on the day shift as the workload was a little heavier during the day. The office was rather small, crammed with three desks, a wall cabinet, a small TV, and only one computer.

After meeting the other translators, Halil excused himself from the tour explaining he had another meeting to get to. From the translator office, Abu Zaid took Fahdi to the office next door, which was the "Americans' office." Inside, Abu Zaid introduced Fahdi to two American guys who both appeared to be in their mid-twenties. The first was a large African-American named Kevin.

"Hey, man, nice to meet you. Welcome to the party," Kevin said flashing a big smile and extending his hand to Fahdi.

The second American, a Caucasian named Jared, was sitting in front of a TV playing a video game. Abu Zaid introduced him to Fahdi. Jared paused his game and stood to shake Fahdi's hand.

"Hey, what game are you playing?" Fahdi asked with a smile.

"Umm, it's called 'Red Faction,'" Jared replied, a little surprised at Fahdi's curiosity. None of the other Iraqi employees had ever asked about their video games.

"Oh, that's a good one," Fahdi commented. "I used to play it a lot with the Marines out at Camp Manhattan."

"Awesome! You're welcome to come over and join us any time. Kevin sucks at this game. It'd be nice to have some competition for a change," Jared said, patting him on the back.

Abu Zaid led Fahdi across the hall to the main Operations Room; a good 1,500 square feet and held twenty small cubicles, each equipped with a computer and manned by an Iraqi employee wearing a set of headphones. As he scanned the room, Fahdi noticed a familiar face seated behind one of the consoles, his brother. Fareed looked up and met Fahdi's gaze, but neither acknowledged the other beyond a silent exchange. At first, Fahdi thought the room was a communications relay station of some sort, then he noticed there were no radios, phones, or any other type of outgoing transmission equipment. The place was completely silent.

"They're just listening," Fahdi remarked half to himself, half to his host.

"Exactly," Abu Zaid replied. "This is the Operator Room. The Americans have them set up with scanners to pick up radio traffic throughout the city. The Operators here listen round-the-clock for anything suspicious. If they come across something they feel is significant, they put it in a memo and pass it to you guys in the translator room. Most of the guys in here don't speak or write in English. It will be your job to translate the memos into English and pass them to the U.S. office. There are always two Americans in the office between the hours of 7 a.m. and 11 p.m. seven days a week. You've met Kevin and Jared, and there are four other Americans that rotate in and out. As of now, the Americans aren't manning their office overnight, but there is talk they may begin to implement an overnight shift since the amount of nighttime activity seems to be increasing here lately."

"What do the Americans do with the information we give them?" Fahdi asked, but immediately realized he'd overstepped.

Abu Zaid smiled. "You translate it and give it to the Americans, that's all you need to know."

Fahdi nodded.

The final stop on the tour was Abu Zaid's private office at the end of the hall across from the translators' office. Inside was a large solid-oak, executive-style desk, as well as a small sofa, a twin bed, a refrigerator, and a small private half bath.

"Looks like you spend quite a bit of time here," Fahdi commented, thinking the room looked more like a motel room than an office.

"I live here," Abu Zaid replied plainly.

Fahdi smiled, thinking it was a joke about the extremely long work hours.

"Seriously," Abu Zaid added, seeing Fahdi didn't believe him. "I relocated my wife and children to Damascus a few months ago, and I now stay here in the building 24/7. I encountered a couple of close calls recently at the hands of some of the insurgency groups here in Baghdad and decided the safest option was to evacuate my family to Syria and for me to remain in the building, until things cool off at least."

Fahdi remained silent, unsure how to respond.

"I know you've dodged a couple of close calls yourself," Abu Zaid continued. "I also know you came to work here hoping to get a break from the chaos and hazards of translating for the U.S. military out in the field. Things are usually quiet here in the building, but I'm sorry to say you shouldn't expect anything to get easier for you out on the street. Stay vigilant and alert outside this building. Vary your routes driving to and from work, and your timing as well. We allow a flexible two-hour window for arrivals and departures, but that doesn't mean you constantly arrive at the tail end of your two-hour window, like some of the little shits here try to pull. You will make more enemies working here; more than you would make had you continued as a terp out in the field. I hope you're prepared for everything that comes along with this new job, the good *and* the negative."

Fahdi returned to the translator office and took a seat at the empty desk, the smallest one right next to the door. Fahdi was the "new kid on the block" and didn't complain. It was so nice to simply sit in a quiet room. Fahdi and the other translators chatted for a while, getting to know each other.

Later in the morning, one of the guys from the Operator Room walked in clutching a small piece of paper. "Here comes a report," Fahdi's fellow translator, Bashir, said as the Operator handed him the paper. "Come over here, I'll show you how to format it for the Americans."

"It wasn't much of a report, only two lines scribbled on half a sheet of notebook paper. I was like, what is it, a riddle or something?"

"The Operators have all been trained on what pertinent information each report needs to include and have been instructed to write it all down in their memo," Bashir explained, "but sometimes they don't have all the info, or they simply forget to put it in the memo. You'll need to double-check with them if anything is missing. The Americans need to know the time the info was intercepted, a list of all names and locations mentioned during the transmission, what frequency they heard it on, and a brief gist of what was said."

Per the note the Operator dropped off, someone talking on a cordless phone indicated he might have seen someone burying an IED next to one of the roads in his neighborhood, but there was no mention of the neighborhood's location. Fahdi deflated, knowing without a location, the intel was basically useless. He'd more than learned his lesson when it came to asking questions or offering suggestions and remained silent. Bashir translated it into English and handed it to Fahdi, telling him to take it over to the Americans. Fahdi went to the adjacent room and knocked on the door of the U.S. office, which was always closed. Kevin answered Fahdi's knock.

"Am I supposed to give you this?" Fahdi asked as Kevin opened the door.

"Awesome, man, thanks. Keep 'em coming," Kevin replied, flashing what Fahdi soon learned was Kevin's trademark big smile.

Fahdi spent the rest of the morning talking with his new co-workers, translating a memo here and there, and was then told to take an hour lunch break. After lunch, he surfed the Internet a little. Bashir had finally vacated his permanent spot in front of the sole computer in the translator office for a couple hours to hang out with some friends in another department. He translated a few more reports dripped in periodically throughout the afternoon and then, before Fahdi knew it, it was time to go home.

I could get used to this.

Finalizing his two-week "probationary period," Abu Zaid called Fahdi into his office for a brief review meeting. After asking how Fahdi's first two weeks of work at the INIS had been and if he had any questions or concerns, Abu Zaid jumped right to his main point of the sit-down.

"The Americans have decided to initiate round-the-clock operations for their team," Abu Zaid explained. "Since they will be here overnight, we are going to need to have a translator on duty at all times as well."

Fahdi knew where Abu Zaid was going with this and acted reluctant to ask.

"I've already spoken with the other translators, but they all have families. None want to work the night shift. I was hoping to have someone volunteer to take the shift and avoid having to force everyone into an equal shift rotation, but it seems—"

"I'll do it," Fahdi impertinently interrupted.

"Are you sure?"

"Will I be the only linguist on the shift?"

"Well, I think we only need one overnight."

"Perfect."

Fahdi, a night owl anyway, was excited to get the office to himself.

No more fighting Bashir for use of the Internet.

Abu Zaid had one of the desks removed from the translator office and replaced it with a small bed. Those on the night shift were allowed to nap. The Operators had instructions to wake them to translate memos.

"Abu Zaid commended me for my 'dedication' and being such a great 'team player' by stepping up to do the night shift. But honestly, it was heaven. Most of the big bosses and managers were gone at night, it was quiet and laid back, and best of all, I wasn't getting shot at or having to spend twelve hours a day riding around in the belly of a sweltering Bradley tank. I got to chill in an air-conditioned office with TV and Internet. Life was good.

"I was fascinated by the internet and spent 95% of my time surfing the web on our office computer. The 'open' internet was relatively new to me, to all Iraqis. Under Saddam, we had the internet, but the government had it strongly regulated. Almost every website was blocked. You couldn't even load *Yahoo!* Unrestricted internet access was a whole new world. I'd spend my nightshifts chatting with random people on *Yahoo! Messenger* and playing a bunch of online games with people in all corners of the world, which I thought was totally cool. We had no clue how vast the internet was and the power it held. It was truly mind blowing.

"On the other hand, because I'd spent the last two years dealing with such a grueling pace and non-stop action, after a few weeks at the INIS, I started to get bored. My new job was less than thrilling and I really missed the guys from the Civil Affairs team. I kept telling myself I should be happy. I'm safe and I work in a clean, comfortable building in the Green Zone. It was everything I'd been dreaming of for months. Yet, I kept feeling like I wasn't where I was supposed to be, something wasn't right, and it definitely wasn't what I wanted to be doing the rest of my life. Typically, like here in the U.S., when you land a government job in Iraq, that's it! You've got it made. Your future is secure and you could bet on being there until you retire, but I needed more. They say you get addicted to the 'high' of adrenalin rushes, especially in a warzone. That's what I was dealing with. Now that I was leading this nine-to-five, cookie cutter existence I felt stifled."

Fahdi did not remain bored for long. His new-found peace and quiet was soon shattered.

CHAPTER EIGHTEEN

THE REST IS HISTORY

JANUARY–MAY 2005

Three months into his new job at the INIS, Fahdi found an envelope taped to the front door of his house. Inside, a handwritten note read, "We know you work for the Americans and coalition forces. This is your warning. Stop working for them now or we will kill you." The envelope also contained a single AK-47 bullet—a clear message. Fahdi burned the letter and didn't mention it to anyone, hoping it to be a one-time occurrence. *Maybe they had the wrong house?* Wishful thinking.

A week later, another note. This time it was typed and wrapped around a hand grenade.

"I guess they had me on an official 'drip campaign' now." Fahdi tried to make light of the situation, but personalized death threats from Al-Qaeda are hard to get over. He sat straighter and rubbed his thighs, a sure sign it bothered him to this day. "What confused me was they were using present tense verbiage.

I figured they thought I was still translating for U.S. troops and had finally caught up with me. But I'd technically already quit working for the Americans and was now employed by the Iraqi government. I hoped they'd figure that out and leave me alone. They were taking the time to leave me notes instead of tracking me down and shooting me in the face. It appeared they only wanted me to meet their demands and be done with it. But how the hell was I supposed to prove to them I wasn't working for the Americans anymore? It's not like I could pick up the phone and call whoever was threatening me to inform them I had quit. I considered writing a reply and taping it to my door for them, but I was worried my mom would find it first. The last thing I wanted was her knowing about the threats. She'd have had a heart attack."

Fahdi took the note with the grenade to the INIS the next day and showed it to Abu Zaid. "First of all," Abu Zaid started, staring wide-eyed at the grenade Fahdi had plopped on his desk, "how the fuck did you get in this building with a grenade?"

"Oh, shit" Fahdi said, genuinely surprised by his own actions. He'd been so preoccupied by his being stalked by the insurgency, he didn't even realize he'd technically waltzed into the Green Zone with a hand grenade. "It was in my bag. Obviously, the guys at the front gate didn't search it very well."

Abu Zaid made a note to have a conversation with the building's security detail. "Are you scared?" Abu Zaid asked, getting back to Fahdi's issue at hand.

"Not really. I have two AKs at my house and I always have my .9mm on me driving to and from work. I'm not going down without a fight."

"So, what do you want us to do?"

"Well, I don't know," Fahdi said, realizing there really was no clear or easy solution. "I'm just letting you know, I guess. But since it's not really safe for me to be going home right now, can I increase my hours here at the building?"

"I don't think any of your fellow translators would mind you picking up a few of their shifts," Abu Zaid replied nonchalantly.

Fahdi upped his nightshifts from five nights a week to seven. The other translators covering the nightshifts on his days off were more than happy to hand them over to Fahdi. He also spent much of the day in the building as well, just hanging out. He'd only leave the building for a couple of hours each day to get food and return home, only long enough to shower and change his clothes. He survived on merely a few hours of sleep each night; whatever he could catch between incoming reports from the Operators.

"I couldn't risk going home to sleep. I was afraid whoever was threatening me would come and kill me in my sleep or hurt my family."

Fahdi even rented a small apartment in a different neighborhood and avoided his mother's house entirely, hoping to divert any negative attention away from his family and perhaps outrun the threats altogether. Nevertheless, he spent his nights in the building in case the insurgents managed to track him down to his new residence.

After a month of practically living in the building and working every night, Fahdi was completely exhausted. Heartened by the fact he'd yet to receive any death threats at his new apartment, he finally decided to take a chance and go home for a few days. His brother reported his mom's house hadn't received any special "notes" since Fahdi had moved out either. He was hopeful whomever had been threatening him had moved on, but he still kept his guard up.

He resumed his normal five-night schedule and spent his two off nights at home, but found he got even less sleep at his apartment than in the building with people waking him up every couple of hours to translate documents. He was even more terrified someone would burst in and attack him while he slept. He dozed for no more than twenty-to thirty-minute stretches, and slept with a loaded pistol—round chambered, safety off—under his pillow and an AK-47 always within arm's reach. Attempting to find some semblance of stability and distract himself from the perils of his daily life, Fahdi reenrolled in Baghdad University, which had recently reopened, to complete his Bachelor's degree in English. Only a semester shy of his degree when the war started, he wanted to finish it up now that he had spare time on his hands. Also, aside from the INIS building, it was the only other place where he felt relatively safe.

"I felt like my life was slowly slipping into a black hole. I was exhausted, both mentally and physically, from living in constant fear, and it seemed there was no light at the end of the tunnel. Even in the middle of a shit storm out in Western Iraq, I always felt like I was at least working toward a goal translating for the military. I had something to look forward to; the reality of 'going home' at some point in time. At the INIS, I no longer felt like I was doing anything worthwhile. I felt invisible there.

"The security situation in Baghdad was deteriorating by the day. When I first started at the INIS, there was a car bomb every couple of weeks or so, then it turned into weekly car bombs, and as we moved into the summer of 2005, the car bombs were a daily occurrence. Traffic across the city was a constant gridlock. It'd take me an hour and a half to drive the five miles between my house and the Green Zone. You'd be sitting in a traffic jam, shots would ring out in the street, and you'd feel like a sitting duck, nowhere to go. You'd just sit and pray that A) you aren't specifically the one being shot at, and B) you don't end up being hit by a stray bullet. I was a ghost. I'm ashamed to say, I even began to rationalize that since I felt dead, why not just make it so. I had nothing left to live for. I'd hit rock bottom."

In May 2005, Fahdi had been functioning in a dazed stupor for a couple of weeks. One afternoon, after his two days off, he walked into the office and immediately felt a strange vibe—strange but good. As if a positive energy had swept through the department. He didn't pay too much attention to it at first, but as the afternoon progressed, he noticed there was a lot of whispering going on and a definitive atmosphere of excitement. An hour into the shift, one of his buddies who worked in the Operator room came into Fahdi's office and plopped down on the small bed next to Fahdi's desk.

"Have you met the new girl yet?"

"What new girl?" Fahdi asked, only half-interested.

"There's a new American girl that started working here yesterday. You haven't seen her?"

"No."

A couple of hours later, there was a knock on the office door and Fahdi called out for whomever it was to come in. In walked Jared from the American team with the "new girl" in tow.

"When I saw her, the air literally left my lungs. I had to fight to keep from vocalizing an obvious gasp to catch my breath. It was the proverbial "lightning bolt." I can't explain it. I just knew, from the minute I saw her, she was the one. Jared introduced us. Her name was Mandy and she'd only been in Iraq for a couple of days. He also told me it was her first deployment to Iraq, which I wasn't surprised to hear. She barely looked old enough to be deploying anywhere. Seventeen? Maybe eighteen? She was actually twenty-two, but she definitely did not look it. Petite with long red hair and blue green eyes. Looking into them, I immediately saw a gentle soul. A warm, bright energy had suddenly appeared in what had become a very cold and dark world for me. I know it sounds cheesy, but Mandy was like the angel who saved me. The day I met her, she saved me from myself. She not only gave me a reason to live but to also hope and dream again. And, of course, two years later, she ultimately got me out of Iraq, saving me in that respect as well.

"After the shock and wonderment subsided, my second thought upon meeting Mandy was, *What the hell is she doing here?* She was totally out of place, so young and innocent. *Why the hell would the Americans send her here to Iraq? Don't they know what this place does to people?* I immediately wanted to protect her. Later, I learned she was a lot tougher than she looked and didn't really need my protection, even in Iraq.

"Jared and Mandy returned to their office and I instantly started brainstorming up an excuse to go over there. I had to see her again. I knew Kevin was there, in the middle of shift change. I got up my nerve, walked over, and struck up a conversation with Kevin. I don't even remember what I said. Words were coming out of my mouth, directed at Kevin, but my eyes were fixed on Mandy, sitting behind one of the two desks in the office. I managed to keep up the mock conversation for a few minutes and then thought it best to excuse myself before anyone got suspicious. I went back to my office, looked at my buddy, and told him, "I'm going to marry that girl."

"And the rest, as they say, is history."

EPILOGUE

Fahdi and I would go on to engage in a love affair ultimately deemed "illicit and scandalous" by both of our governments. He was accused of everything from using me for a Green Card to manipulating me into committing acts of espionage. We defied several government agencies and went through hell in our fight to be together. I was kicked out of the U.S. Navy for refusing to break off my relationship with Fahdi and was forever barred from gaining employment with any U.S. government related entity in the future, but it was all worth it. Our love transcended cultures, countries, and politics, and was the kind of epic romance you typically only read about in storybooks. You *can* read all about how our relationship overcame incredible odds in my Iraq War memoir, *A Foreign Affair*, available from W & B Publishers.

After immigrating to the U.S. in 2007, Fahdi and I were married and welcomed the birth of our first daughter, Elise, in March of 2007. Fahdi was recruited to work as a translator with the U.S. Department of Defense and subsequently returned to Iraq, working yet again on the ground near the front lines with various U.S. military units in the northern part of the country near Mosul. I, like many spouses of military members and civilians who have deployed to Iraq over the years, was home alone raising our child and spending many sleepless nights wondering if my husband was safe. After two years, we decided it simply wasn't worth the risk and hardship anymore. Fahdi resigned from his position and left Iraq behind for good. He essentially had to give up on his country, an emotionally devastating task for him. He'd spent nearly seven years fighting to rebuild Iraq and make it a better place, but it kept slipping deeper and deeper into a chaotic cesspool. The Islamic extremist group ISIS conquered his family's village in Northern Iraq in 2016, leveling an 800-year-old church holding records of Fahdi's familial ancestry dating back to the 12th Century. In a devastating flash, centuries of history was wiped out.

Fahdi's mother, brother, and sister immigrated to the U.S. as refugees in 2009, living with us for a few months in our rural Ohio home before eventually settling in a large Iraqi community outside San Diego. Leaving Iraq was especially difficult on his mother, she'd buried her husband (Fahdi's father) in Iraq and did not want to leave his memory behind. But knowing her children's lives were at risk in Iraq, she too made the difficult decision to walk away from her homeland and much of her family—mother, sisters, brothers—who remain in Iraq today. Fahdi and I welcomed our second daughter, Elaina, in 2014 and celebrated our ten-year wedding anniversary in May of 2017. Although our relationship had an unconventional beginning, we are currently living the "American dream."

We are also doing our best to give back by helping other combat interpreters from Iraq and Afghanistan resettle safely here in the U.S. via the wonderful nonprofit No One Left Behind. The organization was founded by former Army Captain Matt Zeller, whose translator, Janis, saved his life by killing two Taliban insurgents after Zeller and his team were pinned down during a firefight in Afghanistan. There are still thousands of interpreters in Afghanistan and Iraq whose lives are in danger every day due to their service to our military. These heroic veterans fought, bled, and even died alongside our troops on the battlefield. They were our soldiers' eyes and ears on the ground and they are responsible for saving countless American lives. Today they are being systematically targeted and hunted by the Taliban, Al-Qaeda, and other insurgency groups throughout the Middle East. No One Left Behind assists these men and women in obtaining Special Immigrant Visas (SIVs) to come to the U.S. and, once here, helps them find housing, furnishes their apartments, helps them integrate into society, and assists them in finding employment so they can become self-sufficient and productive members of our communities and society. No One Left Behind is helping to ensure America keeps its promise to these interpreters who sacrificed so much for our troops and our missions in Iraq and Afghanistan. To learn more, or if you're interested in volunteering or donating to No One Left behind, please visit www.NoOneLeft.org.

A NOTE TO THE READER

In order to safeguard the privacy and security of the individuals mentioned in this book, all names have been changed. The events recounted here are derived from recorded interviews during which incidents and details were recalled to the best of the interviewee's memory some ten years after their occurrence. All dialogue has been reconstructed and, in some cases, translated from Arabic. Conversations in this book are not verbatim, but are renderings of what was said and what transpired at the time. The views expressed in this book do not represent the views of the Department of Defense or any of its affiliates.

BIBLIOGRAPHY

Krane, Jim. "Translators Dying by the Dozens in Iraq." *Associated Press*, May 2005.

ABOUT THE AUTHOR

Amanda Matti served six years in the US Navy as an intel analyst and is an Iraq War veteran. She is the author of three books. Her memoir, *A Foreign Affair*, tells the story of her 2005 deployment to Baghdad, where she met her husband, an Iraqi national who served as her translator. Her second book, *Voicing the Eagle*, chronicles her husband's story of working as an interpreter for US forces in Iraq. Her latest work, *New Dawn Underground*, is a counter-terrorism thriller about a female CIA analyst who poses as a *Washington Post* journalist to infiltrate a terrorist organization in Iraq. Matti lives in San Diego with her husband, Fahdi, and their two daughters.

OPEN ROAD
INTEGRATED MEDIA

Find a full list of our authors and
titles at www.openroadmedia.com

FOLLOW US
@OpenRoadMedia

www.ingramcontent.com/pod-product-compliance
Lightning Source LLC
Chambersburg PA
CBHW021225090426
42740CB00006B/386